MASON JAR CRAFTS

(UPCYCLE MASON JARS TO KEEP AND GIVE AWAY)

Table of Contents

Introduction

I grew up with mason jars – also known as canning jars – spewed all over my home. Not only did my mom and grandmother use them to store food and in their canning process, but they also used them as cups, candleholders and for storage around the home. So, it's no surprise that I would grow up with a fondness for mason jars. In fact, my fondness is so severe that I have mason jars in various forms in every room of my home. From the living room to the kitchen and even in the bathroom, you cannot escape mason jars in my house!

It seems like I'm not the only one out there, however, with a love of mason jars. A quick search on Google will provide you with thousands, if not millions, of results for recycling those old mason jars. Bloggers have even created websites so they can write about their profound fondness for the mason jar and everything you can turn them into. Even Brides are showing their love for mason jars by incorporating them into their wedding. From the ceremony to the reception, mason jars are making a huge splash in the wedding industry.

The truth is mason jars are a completely versatile and relatively inexpensive item that lasts for many, many years. You can bake in them, turn them into a chandelier, use them as vases or soap dispensers and even display your favorite family photos, all inside a mason jar. What can't you do with mason jars?!

The sheer look of the mason jar coupled with its inexpensive price tag makes them the perfect muse for an abundance of craft projects.

Chapter 1 – Everything you ever Wanted to Know about Mason Jars

The History of Mason Jars

John L. Mason, an inventor from New York City, is credited with inventing the mason jar in 1858. His machine – which he invented – would cut threads into lids. This made a practical way to manufacture reusable jars with screw on lids. The sealing mechanism – a glass jar that has threads molded in its top, zinc lid and sealable rubber ring – is what separated Mr. Mason's design from its predecessors. The patent "Mason's Patent November 30th. 1858" was included on the jars.

The mason jars affordability and ease of use improved the speed of canning. Everyone from farmers to urban families benefited from mason jars. Unfortunately, Mr. Mason sold his rights to his invention to various people and – around 1900 – he died a relatively poor person.

While the term mason jars was once used to describe the jars invented by John Mason, it is now used to describe any type and brand of canning jar. The modern mason jar is manufactured by many different companies, with Jarden Home Brands being one of the most popular. They make the Ball and Kerr brands that most people are familiar with.

Mason Jars and Their Varying Sizes

Mason jars are available in a wide array of sizes and styles. Regular or wide mouth, half-pint, pint, quart, half-gallon and gallon are some of the most popular types. There are even jelly jars, which are typically smaller than other types of mason jars.

The smallest jelly jar has the capacity to hold no more than 4-ounces.

The most common mason jar is made from clear glass. However, there are some jars with green or blue tinted glass. There are even mason jars in hues of yellow, amber and olive, although these colors are generally hard to find.

Where to Find Mason Jars

Mason jars are readily available at department and grocery stores around the world. They are typically located in the canning section. During canning season – which is usually in spring or summer –, the availability of mason jars can become scarce. You should take this into consideration when planning your mason jar crafts.

Before you run out and buy brand new mason jars, however, why not try to round up some old jars from family and friends who may not want them. Make sure to inform them that the mason jars will be used for craft purposes and that you won't be returning them. This will help prevent any hard feelings if they assume you will be giving the mason jars back when you're finished with them.

Another option is to scour yard sales, flea markets and thrift stores. It is not uncommon to find old and really cheap mason jars at these locations. Keep in mind, however, that a lot of used mason jars won't have the lids and rings included, and you may have to purchase new lids and rings if they are required for the craft project.

Chapter 2 – Preparing the Jars: How to Get the Mason Jars Ready for your Project

Before you begin any mason jar craft project, you must first prepare the jars. Even if the jars are brand new, you will need to clean them thoroughly. This will get rid of any dust, dirt or debris that could be on or inside the jars.

To clean the mason jars, lay a dishtowel along the bottom of the sink. This dishtowel will help to protect the jars from the hard bottom. Fill the sink up with warm soapy water. Gently and thoroughly wash each jar individually. Rinse the jars with cool water to remove soapy residue and let air dry. Don't forget to also thoroughly wash the mason jar lids and rings in warm soapy water as well. If you prefer, you can also wash them in the dishwasher.

Some people like to sterilize the jars before using. I only sterilize my mason jars when I first purchase them new or if I get them used. If you prefer to sterilize the jars, simply place the clean jars in a large pot. Make sure the jars are place right side up. Pour enough water in the pot so that the jars are completely covered. Place the pot on the stove and bring the water to a rolling boil. Allow the water to boil for about 15 minutes. Turn the heat off and toss in the canning lids. Let the jars and lids sit in the water for anywhere from 10 minutes to 1 hour. Use tongs to carefully remove the lids and jars from the water, drying each one thoroughly with a lint-free cloth. Use the sterilized jars immediately for your craft project or place in a safe location.

Chapter 3 – Gift Jar Recipes

Chocolate Gift Jars

Brownie Cake Gift Jar

Ingredients:

- 2 pint-sized wide-mouth mason jars
- 1 cup flour, all-purpose
- 1 cup granulated sugar
- ½ teaspoon baking soda
- ¼ teaspoon ground cinnamon
- 1/3 cup margarine or butter
- 3 tablespoons unsweetened cocoa powder
- ¼ cup water
- ¼ cup buttermilk
- 1 egg, beaten
- ½ teaspoon vanilla extract
- ¼ cups finely chopped walnuts

Directions:

Step 1: Turn the oven to 325-degrees Fahrenheit to preheat.

Step 2: Mix the flour, baking soda, sugar and cinnamon together in a small mixing bowl. Set the bowl aside for the moment.

Step 2: Combine the margarine or butter, cocoa powder and water together in a medium saucepan. Stir together until the margarine or butter has melted and the ingredients are well blended.

Step 3: Remove the melted ingredients from heat and stir in the flour mixture.

Step 4: Stir in the buttermilk, egg and vanilla. Beat the mixture with a whisk until it is smooth.

Step 5: Stir the walnuts into the mixture.

Step 6: Carefully pour the mixture into two 1-pint mason jars with wide mouths. Set the jars on a cookie sheet and place inside the oven.

Step 7: Bake the brownie cakes in the oven at 325-degrees for 35 to 40 minutes, or when a toothpick inserted into the brownie comes out clean.

Step 8: With an oven mitt, remove the brownie cakes from the oven and set on a cooling rake.

Step 9: Immediately place the lid and ring onto each mason jar. Screw the ring down tightly.

Step 10: Leave the brownie cakes to cool for a few hours. You should hear a pop or plink sound. This is the ring sealing onto the mason jar. If you don't hear that sound, simply press down on the middle of the lids after the brownie cakes have cooled.

Step 11: Store the brownie cakes in a cool, dark area. If stored properly, the brownie cakes will last up to a year.

M&M Cookie Mix Gift Jar

Ingredients:

- 1 quart-sized wide-mouth mason jar
- 1 ¼ cup granulated sugar
- 1 ¼ cup M&Ms
- 2 cups flour, all-purpose
- ½ teaspoon baking powder
- ½ teaspoon baking soda

Directions:

Step 1: In a small bowl, mix the flour, baking powder and baking soda together.

Step 2: Pour the granule sugar into a 1-quart, wide-mouth mason jar.

Step 3: Pour the M&Ms directly on top of the sugar.

Step 4: Pour the flour mixture directly on top of the M&Ms. Press the flour mixture down into the jar tightly with clean fingers.

Step 5: Screw the lid and ring onto the jar. Cover the top of the lid with a decorative piece of fabric and tie with a matching ribbon.

Chocolate Gift Jar Cakes

Ingredients:

- 8 pint-sized, wide-mouth mason jars
- 1 stick + 3 tablespoons butter, unsalted
- 3 cups granulated sugar
- 4 large eggs
- 1 tablespoon vanilla
- 2 cups applesauce, unsweetened
- 3 cups flour, all-purpose
- ¼ cup unsweetened cocoa powder
- ½ teaspoon baking powder
- 1 teaspoon baking soda
- 1/8 teaspoon salt

Directions:

Step 1: Preheat the oven on 325-degrees Fahrenheit.

Step 2: Grease the inside of the mason jar thoroughly with cooking spray or vegetable oil.

Step 3: Beat the butter and 1 ½ cups of sugar together until fluffy.

Step 4: Add the eggs, remaining 1 ½ cups of sugar, applesauce and vanilla. Continuing beating until well combined.

Step 5: Mix the flour, cocoa powder, baking powder, baking soda and salt together.

Step 6: Add the flour mixture to the sugar/butter mixture a little at a time. Make sure to thoroughly beat the mixture after each addition. Continue in this manner until you have incorporated the entire flour mixture into the sugar/butter mixture.

Step 7: Carefully pour a cup of the cake batter into each mason jar. Wipe any batter off the rims of the jar with a paper towel.

Step 8: Set the mason jars on a cookie sheet and bake in the oven for about 40 minutes.

Step 9: While the cakes are baking in the oven, bring a pot of water to a boil. Add the jar lids and remove from heat. You must make sure the lids stay hot until placed on the jars.

Step 10: When the cakes are done baking, carefully remove them from the oven with an oven mitt and place on a cooling rake.

Step 11: Place the lids on the jars and secure them closed with the rings. Make sure the jar rims are clean before placing the lids on. If not clean, the jars won't seal properly.

Step 12: Let cook for several hours. As long as the jars remain sealed, they should last for a year. However, for best flavor, the canned cakes should be consumed within 6-months.

S'Mores Gift Jar

Ingredients:

- 1 quart-sized mason jar
- 1 ½ cups crushed graham crackers
- 1 package of seasonal Peeps marshmallow candies
- 1/3 cup brown sugar, packed
- 1 ¼ cup chocolate chips or M&Ms

Directions:

Step 1: Dump the crushed graham crackers into the mason jar. With a meat tenderizer, pack the crushed graham cracker tightly into the bottom of the mason jar.

Step 2: Place the marshmallow Peeps into the jar on top of the crushed graham crackers. Use about 2/3 of the package. Press the Peeps lightly against the glass. This will create a hole or well in the center of the mason jar.

Step 3: Pour the brown sugar in the hole or well created in Step 2. Gently press down on the brown sugar with your fingers to pack it a bit.

Step 4: Pour the chocolate chips or M&Ms into the jar. Secure the lid and ring onto the mason jar.

Step 5: Decorate the jar with fabric and ribbon. Attach a gift tag to the jar that has the following information written on it:

S'Mores Gift Jar Recipe

1. Preheat an oven to 350-degrees Fahrenheit.

2. Dump the contents of the jar into a large mixing bowl. Remove the marshmallow Peeps. Mix the remaining ingredients together.

3. Cut the marshmallow Peeps into small pieces. Place back into the bowl and stir the ingredients together.

4. In a microwave-safe bowl, melt ½ cup of butter. Add 1/3 cup buttermilk and 1 teaspoon vanilla extract to the melted butter and stir until mixed well.

5. Pour the melted butter mixture into the bowl containing the dry ingredients. Mix until all ingredients are incorporated into one another.

6. Lightly grease a 9-by-9 pan. Press the cookie batter into the greased pan and bake for 15 minutes.

Peppermint Brownie Mix Gift Jar

- Mason jar
- 2/3 cup cocoa powder, unsweetened
- 2 cups sugar
- 1 cup Andes peppermint crunch baking chips
- 1 ¼ cup all-purpose flour
- Pinch of table salt

Directions:

Step1: Pour the cocoa powder into the mason jar. Layer 1 cup of sugar on top.

Step 2: Add the peppermint baking chips. Pour 1 cup of sugar on top of the peppermint chips.

Step 3: Mix the flour and the salt together in a bowl. Pour the mixture carefully on top of the sugar layer.

Step 4: Secure the lid and ring onto the mason jar. Attach a label with the following baking instructions:

1. Preheat oven to 350-degrees.
2. Pour the contents of the jar into a mixing bowl.
3. Melt 1 cup (2 sticks) of butter and mix into the dry ingredients.
4. Add 2 teaspoons vanilla and 4 eggs. Mix thoroughly.
5. Pour the batter into a greased 9-inch by 13-inch pan. Bake for about 25 minutes.

Dessert Gift Jars

Toffee Blondie Bars Mix Gift Jar

Ingredients:

- 1 quart-sized mason jar
- 1 cup all-purpose flour
- ¼ teaspoon salt
- 1 teaspoon baking powder
- ½ cup mini chocolate chips
- 1 cup brown sugar, packed
- ½ cup Heath toffee chips
- ¾ cup rice crisp cereal

Directions:

Step 1: Combine the flour, salt and baking powder together in a small bowl.

Step 2: Pour the flour mixture into the mason jar.

Step 3: Layer the remaining ingredients in the mason jar.

Step 4: Attach a label or tag to the jar that has the following baking instructions:

1. Preheat oven to 350 degrees.
2. Lightly grease an 8x8 pan.
3. In a mixing bowl, add 2 lightly beaten eggs, ¼ cup of softened butter and 1 teaspoon of vanilla. Mix the 3 ingredients together until it becomes fluffy.
4. Pour the entire jar into the mixing bowl. Mix until well blended.
5. Pour the batter into the greased pan.
6. Bake for 25 to 30 minutes or until the bars have set.

7. Let cool in the pan before cutting.

Pumpkin Cranberry Bread Mix Gift Jar

Ingredients:

- 1 quart-sized mason jar
- 1 ½ cups all-purpose flour
- 1 ½ teaspoons pumpkin pie spice
- ½ teaspoon baking soda
- ½ teaspoon baking powder
- ½ teaspoon salt
- 1 cup white sugar
- 1/3 cup packed brown sugar
- ½ cup rolled oats
- ¾ cup dried cranberries

Directions:

Step 1: In a small bowl, combine the flour, pumpkin pie spice, baking soda, baking powder and salt together.

Step 2: Pour the flour mixture into the mason jar. Layer the remaining ingredients in the mason jar.

Step 3: Secure the lid and ring onto the mason jar. Attach a tag or label to the jar with the following baking instructions:

1. Preheat oven to 350-degrees. Grease and flour 2 medium-sized loaf pans.
2. In a mixing bowl, combine ½ cup vegetable oil, 1 cup canned pumpkin and 2 large eggs. Continue mixing until well blended. Set the mixing bowl aside.

3. In a second mixing bowl, pour out the contents of the mason jar. Mix the dry ingredients until thoroughly combined.
4. Pour the dry ingredients into the oil/pumpkin mixture. Stir until well blended.
5. Evenly divide the batter between the 2 loaf pans.
6. Bake for 40 to 50 minutes or when a toothpick inserted into the middle of the bread comes out clean.

Chocolate Chip Banana Bread Mix Gift Jar

Ingredients:

- 1 quart-sized mason jar
- 2 ½ cups Bisquick
- ¼ teaspoon salt
- 1 teaspoon baking powder
- ½ cup white sugar
- ½ cups finely chopped dried bananas
- ½ cup chocolate chips

Directions:

Step 1: Combine the Bisquick, salt and baking powder in a bowl.

Step 2: Pour the mixture into the mason jar. Layer the sugar, dried bananas and chocolate chips into the jar.

Step 3: Place the lid and ring on the mason jar. Attach a tag or label with the following baking instructions:

1. Preheat the oven to 350-degrees. Grease a large loaf pan and cover the bottom with wax paper.
2. Pour the contents of the mason jar into a large bowl. Push the dry ingredients along the side of the bowl to create a well in the middle.
3. Add 1 1/4 cup milk, 2 lightly beaten eggs, 1/2 cup of softened butter and 1 teaspoon vanilla extract into the well.
4. Mix all the ingredients together until well blended.

5. Transfer the batter to the large loaf pan and bake for about an hour or until a toothpick inserted into the middle of the bread comes out clean.
6. Let cool before enjoying.

No-Bake Holiday Chex Mix Gift Jar

Ingredients:

- Mason jar
- Holiday fabric
- Twine
- Candy cane
- Chex Mix Muddy Buddies
- 1 box chocolate Chex Mix cereal
- 1 bag mini pretzel twists
- 1 bag holiday M&Ms

Directions:

Step 1: Pour the Muddy Buddies, chocolate Chex Mix cereal, pretzels and M&Ms into a large bowl. Mix with a spoon until well blended.

Step 2: Pour the mixture into the mason jar.

Step 3: Cut a circle that measures about 5 ¼-inch in diameter from the Holiday fabric.

Step 4: Place the lid on top of the mason jar. Lay the circle-shaped fabric on top of the lid. Screw the ring onto the jar over the fabric.

Step 5: Attach the candy cane to the jar with a piece of twine.

Cinnamon Spice Muffin Mix Gift Jar

Ingredients:

- 1-quart mason jar
- Cupcake liners
- Twine
- 2 ½ cups all-purpose flour
- ¾ cup sugar
- ½ teaspoon baking soda
- 2 teaspoons baking powder
- ½ teaspoon salt
- 1 ½ teaspoons ground cinnamon
- ¼ teaspoon ground ginger
- ¼ teaspoon ground nutmeg
- ¼ teaspoon ground cloves
- ½ cup brown sugar, packed
- Baggie

Directions:

Step 1: In a mixing bowl, combine 1 cups of flour, sugar, baking soda, baking powder, salt, cinnamon, ginger, nutmeg and cloves together.

Step 2: Pour the flour mixture into the mason jar.

Step 3: In a small mixing bowl, combine ½ cup flour and brown sugar together. Transfer the mixture into a baggie. Tie the baggie closed with a knot. Lay the baggie on top of the flour mixture.

Step 4: Secure the lid and ring onto the jar.

Step 5: Attach a label or tag to the jar with the following baking instructions:

1. Preheat oven to 400-degrees.
2. Empty the baggie into a small bowl. Add ¼ cup of butter and mix to create a crumb topping for the muffins. Set aside for the moment.
3. Pour the remaining ingredients in the jar into a mixing bowl.
4. Stir in ¼ cup oil, 1 cup milk, 1 egg and 1 teaspoon of vanilla. Continuing stirring until all ingredients are incorporated into one another.
5. Line a muffin tin with the included cupcake liners.
6. Spoon the batter into the liners. Sprinkle the crumb topping on the top of the batter.
7. Bake the muffins for about 15 minutes.

Step 6: Place a stack of cupcake liners on top of the mason jar. Secure the liners in place with twine.

Blueberry Muffin Mix Gift Jar

Ingredients:

- 1 quart-sized mason jar
- 2 cups all-purpose flour
- 1 ¼ cups + 2 teaspoons sugar, divided
- ½ teaspoon salt
- 2 teaspoons baking powder
- Cupcake liners
- Ribbon

Directions:

Step 1: Mix the flour, sugar, salt and baking powder together in a bowl.

Step 2: Pour the mixture into the mason jar. Secure the lid and ring on to the jar.

Step 3: Place the cupcake liners on top of the mason jar. Secure the liners in place with the ribbon.

Step 4: Attach a label or tag to the jar with the following baking instructions:

1. Preheat oven to 350-degrees.
2. Dump the mason jar into a mixing bowl.
3. Mix in 2 eggs and ½ cup melted butter. Fold in 2 ½ cups of fresh blueberries.
4. Place the cupcake liners in the muffin pan. Spoon the batter into the liners.
5. Bake in the oven for 25 to 30 minutes, or when the muffins are golden brown and puffy.

Cookie Gift Jars

Gingerbread Cookie Mix

Ingredients:

- 1 quart-sized mason jar
- 1 ½ cup flour
- 1 teaspoon baking soda
- 1 teaspoon baking powder
- ½ teaspoon salt
- ½ cup brown sugar
- 2 teaspoon ginger
- 1 teaspoon cinnamon
- ½ teaspoon allspice
- ¼ teaspoon cloves
- 1 ½ cup flour
- ½ cup brown sugar

Directions:

Step 1: In the mason jar, layer the ingredients as listed above.

Step 2: Secure the lid and ring onto the mason jar. Tie a gingerbread man cookie cutter to the jar.

Step 3: On a decorative tag, write the following instructions:

1. Cream together1 stick (1/2 cup butter), 1 egg and ¾ cup molasses in a mixing bowl.
2. Add the gingerbread cookie mix and blend well. Cover the mixture and place in the refrigerator for an hour.
3. On a lightly floured surface, roll the chilled dough out to about ¼-inch.
4. Use the cookie cutter to cut out the gingerbread shape from the dough. Place the cookies on a greased cookie sheet.

5. Bake the cookies at 350-degrees for about 10 to 12 minutes.

Cranberry Winter Cookie Mix Gift Jar

Ingredients:

- 1 quart-sized mason jar
- 1 cup + 2 tablespoons all-purpose flour
- ½ teaspoon salt
- ½ teaspoon baking soda
- ½ cup rolled oats
- 1/3 cup white sugar
- 1/3 cup packed brown sugar
- ½ cup dried cranberries
- ½ cup white chocolate chips
- ½ cups chopped pecans

Directions:

Step 1: In a small bowl, mix the flour, salt and baking soda together. Set them to the side.

Step 2: Layer flour mixture, rolled oats, white sugar, brown sugar, cranberries, white chocolate chips and chopped pecans in the mason jar.

Step 3: Secure the lid and ring on the jar.

Step 4: Secure a label or tag to the jar that has the following baking instructions:

1. Preheat the oven to 350-degrees Fahrenheit. Grease the bottom of a cookie sheet or line the cookie sheet with parchment paper.
2. In a large mixing bowl, cream together ½ cup of softened butter, 1 large egg and 1 teaspoon of vanilla until the three ingredients are fluffy.

3. Pour the cookie mix into the mixing bowl and stir until well blended.
4. Scoop the cookie dough onto the baking sheet.
5. Bake the cookies for about 8 to 10 minutes or until their edges start to turn brown.
6. Let the cookies cool on a wire rack.

Santa's Cookie Mix Gift Jar

Ingredients:

- 1 quart-sized mason jar
- 1 1/3 cup all-purpose flour
- 1 teaspoon baking soda
- 1 teaspoon baking powder
- ¼ teaspoon salt
- 1 cup rolled oats
- ¾ cup M&Ms candies
- ½ cup packed brown sugar
- ½ cup white sugar
- ¼ to ¾ cup semi-sweet chocolate chips

Directions:

Step 1: In a small mixing bowl, combine the flour, baking soda, baking powder and salt together.

Step 2: Pour the flour mixture into the mason jar. Layer the oats, M&Ms, brown sugar, white sugar and semi-sweet chocolate chips in the mason jar.

Step 3: Secure the lid and ring on the mason jar. Attach a label or tag onto the jar that has the following baking instructions:

1. Preheat oven to 350-degrees. Grease the bottom of a cookie sheet or line the cookie sheet with parchment paper.
2. In a large mixing bowl, cream together ½ cup of softened butter, 1 large egg and 1 teaspoon of vanilla until the three ingredients are fluffy.
3. Pour the cookie mix into the mixing bowl and stir until well blended.

4. Roll the cookie dough into 1 ½-inch balls and place on the cookie sheet.
5. Bake the cookies for about 10 minutes or until their edges start to turn brown.
6. Let the cookies cool on a wire rack.

Reese's Chocolate Cookie Mix Gift Jar

Ingredients:

- 1 quart-sized wide-mouth mason jar
- 1 box super moist milk chocolate cake mix
- 1 bag Reese's mini pieces peanut butter baking chips

Directions:

Step 1: Open the chocolate cake mix and pour the contents into the mason jar. Pat the top of the mix gently.

Step 2: Pour the Reese's mini pieces directly on top of the mix.

Step 3: Secure the lid and ring on the jar. Attach a label or tag to the jar with the following baking instructions:

1. Preheat the oven at 350-degrees.
2. Beat 2 large eggs and ½ cup oil – canola or vegetable – in a mixing bowl.
3. Dump the contents of the mason jar into the mixing bowl. Stir until well incorporated.
4. Place dough in the fridge for about 15 minutes to chill.
5. Roll the dough into small 1 1/2 –inch balls and place on a cookie sheet.
6. Bake the cookies for about 8 to 9 minutes.

Oatmeal and Chocolate Chip Cookie Mix Gift Jar

Ingredients:

- 1 quart-sized mason jar
- ¾ cup all-purpose flour
- ½ teaspoon salt
- ¼ teaspoon baking soda
- 1 teaspoon ground cinnamon
- 1 ½ cups quick cooking oats
- ½ cup semi-sweet chocolate chips
- ½ cup packed brown sugar
- ¼ cup white sugar

Directions:

Step 1: Combine the flour, salt, baking soda and cinnamon together in a bowl.

Step 2: Pour the flour mixture into the mason jar.

Step 3: Layer the oats, chocolate chips, brown sugar and white sugar on top of the flour mixture.

Step 4: Place the lid on the mason jar and screw the ring on tight.

Step 5: Attach a tag or label to the jar with the following baking instructions:

1. Preheat oven to 325-degrees.
2. Mix 1 cup of softened butter, 1 egg and 1 teaspoon of vanilla in a bowl.
3. Pour the contents of the jar into the bowl and mix until well combined.

4. Drop spoonfuls of the cookie dough onto a cookie sheet and bake for 12 minutes.
5. Remove the cookies from the cookie sheet and let cool on a wire rake.

Christmas Mint Cookie Mix Gift Jar

Ingredients:

- 1 quart-sized mason jar
- 2 ½ cup all-purpose flour
- 1 teaspoon baking soda
- 1 teaspoon baking powder
- 1 teaspoon salt
- ¾ cup white sugar
- ¾ cup packed brown sugar
- ½ cup green and red M&M's
- ¼ cup peppermint candies, crushed

Directions:

Step 1: Mix the flour, baking soda, baking powder and salt together in a bowl. Pour the mixture into the mason jar.

Step 2: Pour the white sugar on top of the flower mixture. Add the brown sugar. Using the back of a spoon, tamp down on the brown sugar.

Step 3: Layer the M&M's on top of the brown sugar, followed by the crushed peppermint candies.

Step 4: Secure the lid and ring on the mason jar. Attach a label or tag to the jar with the following baking instructions:

1. Pour the contents of the jar into a large mixing bowl.
2. Add 1 large egg and 1 tablespoon of vanilla. Mix until well incorporated.
3. Beat in 1 stick of butter (softened).
4. Cover the bowl with cling film and place in the fridge for about an hour to chill.

5. Preheat oven to 350 degrees. Remove the cookie dough from the fridge. Cover a cookie sheet with parchment paper.
6. Roll dough into 1 to 2 inch balls. Place the dough balls on the cookie sheet.

Bake the cookies for about 15 to 18 minutes. Let the cookies cool on a wire rack.

Chocolate Chip Cookie Mix Gift Jar

Ingredients:

- 1 quart-sized mason jar
- 1 2/3 cups all-purpose flour
- ¾ teaspoon baking soda
- ½ cup white sugar
- 1 ½ cup semi-sweet chocolate chips
- ½ cup brown sugar

Directions:

Step 1: Combine the flour baking soda and white sugar together in a mixing bowl.

Step 2: Pour 1/3 cup of the flour/sugar mixture into the mason jar.

Step 3: Layer the chocolate chips on top of the flour mixture, followed by the brown sugar. Use the back of a spoon to press down on the brown sugar.

Step 4: Pour the remaining flour mixture into the mason jar. Secure the jar closed with the lid and ring.

Step 5: Write the following baking instructions on a label that you will attach to the top of the mason jar:

1. Preheat oven to 375-degrees.
2. Empty the mason jar into a large mixing bowl. Set aside for the moment.
3. In a smaller mixing bowl, cream ¾ cup of softened butter, 1 teaspoon vanilla extract and 2 large eggs.
4. Scoop the butter mixture into the large mixing bowl with the cookie mix.

5. Stir the mixture until well combined.
6. Scoop the cookie dough by spoonfuls and drop onto a cookie sheet (ungreased).
7. Bake the cookies for about 8 to 10 minutes or until the edges begin to lightly brown.
8. Remove the cookies from the cookie sheet and let cool on a wire rake.

Reindeer Cookie Mix Gift Jar

Ingredients:

- 1 quart-sized mason jar
- ½ cup unbleached flour
- ½ cup whole wheat flour
- 1 teaspoon baking soda
- 1 teaspoon baking powder
- 1 teaspoon salt
- 1 cup quick oats
- ¾ cup M&M's candies
- ¾ cup semi-sweet chocolate chips
- ½ cup packed brown sugar
- ½ cup white sugar
- ½ cup pecans, chopped

Directions:

Step 1: Mix the flours, baking soda, baking powder and salt together in a bowl.

Step 2: In the mason jar, layer the ingredients in this order: flour mixture, oats, M&M's, chocolate chips, brown sugar, white sugar and chopped pecans. Pack the ingredients down after adding each layer.

Step 3: Place the lid on the jar and screw on the ring. Attach a label or tag to the jar that includes the following baking directions:

1. Preheat oven to 350-degrees.

2. Add ½ cup of butter (softened, 1 large egg (slightly beaten) and 1 teaspoon of vanilla to a large mixing bowl.
3. Dump the cookie mix into the bowl and mix until the ingredients are well combined.
4. Cover a cookie sheet with parchment paper.
5. Roll the cookie dough into 1-inch balls. Place the dough balls on the parchment-covered cookie sheet.
6. Bake the dough for about10 minutes.

Butterscotch Chip Cookie Mix Gift Jar

Ingredients:

- 1 quart-sized wide mouth mason jar
- 1 box butter recipe yellow cake mix (15.25 ounce)
- 1 package butterscotch morsels (11 ounce)

Directions:

Step 1: Pour the yellow cake mix into the mason jar. Pour the package of butterscotch morsels on top of the cake mix.

Step 2: Attach a label or tag to the mason jar with the following baking instructions:

1. Preheat the oven on 350-degrees.
2. Beat 2 large eggs in a medium-sized mixing bowl. Add canola or vegetable oil and blend until well mixed.
3. Pour the contents of the jar into the mixing bowl. Stir with a spoon.
4. Place the dough into the fridge for about 15 minutes.
5. Drop rounded spoonfuls of the cookie dough onto a cookie sheet (ungreased).
6. Bake the cookies for about 8 to 9 minutes.

Triple Chocolate Cookie Mix Gift Jar

Ingredients:

- 1 quart-sized wide mouth mason jar
- 1 box triple chocolate cake mix (15.25 ounce)
- 1 cup semi-sweet chocolate chips

Directions:

Step 1: Pour the chocolate cake mix into the mason jar. Pour the 1 cup of semi-sweet chocolate chips on top of the cake mix.

Step 2: Attach a label or tag to the mason jar with the following baking instructions:

1. Preheat the oven on 350-degrees.
2. Beat 2 large eggs in a medium-sized mixing bowl. Add canola or vegetable oil and blend until well mixed.
3. Pour the contents of the jar into the mixing bowl. Stir with a spoon.
4. Place the dough into the fridge for about 15 minutes.
5. Drop rounded spoonfuls of the cookie dough onto a cookie sheet (ungreased).
6. Bake the cookies for about 8 to 9 minutes.

Soup in a Jar

<u>Hearty Soup Mix Gift Jar</u>

Ingredients:

- 1 quart-sized mason jar
- 1/3 cup chicken or beef bouillon cubes
- ¼ cup onion flakes
- ½ cup split peas
- ½ cup elbow macaroni or small shell pasta
- ¼ cup barley
- ¼ cup lentils
- ¼ cup rice
- Spiral pasta, multi color

Directions:

Step 1: Layer the ingredients in the order given above in the mason jar. Fill the remaining space with the multi color spiral pasta.

Step 2: Write the following recipe on a tag and attach it to the mason jar:

Hearty Soup Recipe

1. Brown 1 pound of ground beef and drain. Set to the side.
2. Remove the spiral multi color pasta and set aside for the moment.
3. Add 12 to 14 cups of water to a large pot and place on the stove.
4. Dump the ingredients remaining in the mason jar into the pot of water.

5. Bring the water to a boil and let simmer for about 45 minutes.
6. Add the spiral multi color pasta and let simmer for 15 minutes.
7. Add the browned beef to the soup and serve.

Soup in a Jar Gift

Ingredients:

- 1 quart wide-mouth mason jar
- ½ cup dried split peas
- ½ cup barley
- ½ cup dry lentils
- ½ cup uncooked rice
- 2 tablespoons dried minced onion
- 2 teaspoons salt
- 2 tablespoons dried parsley
- ½ teaspoon lemon pepper
- 2 tablespoons beef bouillon granules
- ½ cup alphabet pasta, uncooked
- 1 cup twist macaroni, uncooked

Directions:

Step 1: Layer the split peas, barley, lentils and rice in the mason jar.

Step 2: Layer the onion, salt, parsley, lemon pepper, beef bouillon and uncooked alphabet pasta around the edges of the jar.

Step 3: Fill the remaining free space in the jar with twist macaroni.

Step 4: Secure the lid and ring on the mason jar.

Step 5: Attach a tag with the following recipe on the jar:

1. Pour the contents of the mason jar into a pot filled with 3 quarts water. Add 2 sliced carrots, 2 stalks chopped celery, 2 cups diced tomatoes and 1 cup shredded cabbage.
2. Place the pot on the stove, cover and simmer over medium low heat for about an hour or until the vegetables become tender.

Love Soup Mix Gift Jar

Ingredients:

- 1 quart wide-mouth mason jar
- 1/3 cup beef bouillon granules
- ¼ cup dried minced onion
- ½ cup dried split peas
- ½ cup twist macaroni, uncooked
- ¼ cup barley
- ½ cup dry lentils
- 1/3 cup long grain white rice
- 1 cup tri-color spiral pasta, uncooked

Directions:

Step 1: Layer the bouillon, onion flakes, split peas, twist macaroni, barley, dry lentils and white rice.

Step 2: Pour enough spiral pasta into the mason jar so that it is completely filled.

Step 3: Write the following cooking instructions on a tag:

1. Brown 1 pound of ground beef. Drain and set aside.
2. Remove the spiral pasta from the mason jar and set aside.
3. Pour the remaining ingredients into a pot filled with 12 cups of water.
4. Place the pot on the stove. Let the contents come to a boil before turning the heat down and allowing the soup to simmer for 45 minutes.
5. Add the spiral pasta to the soup and let simmer for an additional 15 minutes.

6. Add the browned ground beef. Serve the soup warm with a tossed salad, dinner rolls or bread sticks.

Curried Lentil Soup Mix Gift Jar

Ingredients:

- ¾ liter mason jar
- 2 bay leaves
- 1 Chile pepper, dried
- 2 teaspoons turmeric
- 1 ½ teaspoon curry powder
- 5 sun-dried tomatoes
- ½ cup yellow lentils
- ½ cup red lentils
- ½ cup yellow lentils
- ½ cup red lentils

Directions:

Step 1: Layer the ingredients in the order outlined above in a mason jar.

Step 2: Attach the following recipe to the mason jar:

Curried Lentil Soup Instructions

1. Place 3 tablespoons of butter in a pot and heat over medium heat.
2. Smash 4 garlic cloves and place them in the pot. Add 1 diced red onion. Sauté for about 6 minutes.
3. Pour the curry powder, Chile pepper and bay leaves into the pot. Let cook for about 3 minutes.
4. Add 8 cups of water and the remaining ingredients into the pot and summer for about an hour or until the lentils are soft.

5. Season to taste with salt if desired.

Vegetarian Five Bean Soup Gift Jar

Ingredients:

- 4 quart-sized mason jars
- 1 pound split green peas
- 1 pound pinto beans
- 1 pound great northern beans
- 1 pound kidney beans
- 1 pound black beans
- 1 tablespoon paprika
- 1 tablespoon black pepper
- 1 tablespoon dry mustard
- 2 tablespoons dehydrated onions
- 2 tablespoons garlic powder
- 2 tablespoons sea salt
- 2 tablespoons dried oregano
- 1 teaspoon dried rosemary
- 8 bay leaves
- 4 vegetable bouillon cubes

Directions:

Step 1: Layer 2/3 cup pinto beans in each one of the mason jars. Gently shake the jar to level the pinto beans. Repeat the process with 2/3 cup green peas, 2/3 cup great northern beans and 2/3 cup kidney beans. Set the jars to the side for the moment.

Step 2: Combine the remaining ingredients – except the bouillon cubes and bay leaves -- together in a mixing bowl.

Step 3: Lay 4 pieces of parchment paper that measures about 10-inches x 10-inches. Pour 3 tablespoons of the mixture from

Step 2 in the middle of each parchment paper. Lay one bouillon cube and two bay leaves on top of the spices.

Step 4: Fold the filled parchment paper around the ingredients to create a spice packet. Seal the packet with tape. Press the packet into the mason jar and secure the jar closed with the lid and ring.

Step 5: Write the desired cooking instructions neatly on a label and attach to the mason jars.

Chicken Noodle Soup Gift Jar

Ingredients:

- 1 quart-sized mason jar
- 2 tablespoons minced onion
- 2 tablespoons chicken bouillon granules
- 2 teaspoons dried celery
- 1 teaspoon pepper
- 4 cups wide egg noodles

Directions:

Step 1: layer the mason jar with the minced onion, followed by the chicken bouillon granules, dried celery and pepper.

Step 2: Pack the wide egg noodles directly on top of the spices. Secure the mason jar closed with a lid and ring.

Step 3: Write the cooking instructions on a tag and attach it to the jar.

Texas 2-Step Soup Mix Gift Jar

Ingredients:

- 1 pint-sized wide-mouth mason jar
- 1 brown gravy mix package, 1.61 ounce
- 2 teaspoons dried oregano
- 2 tablespoons chili powder
- 1 teaspoon dried minced onion
- 1 teaspoon ground cumin
- ½ teaspoon garlic salt
- 12 tortilla chips, crushed
- 1 ¼ cups pasta shells

Directions:

Step 1: Pour the gravy mix into the mason jar. Set a side.

Step 2: Mix the chili powder, cumin, garlic salt, onion and oregano in a bowl. Pour the spice mix directly on top of the gravy.

Step 3: Place the crushed tortilla chips on top of the spices, followed by the pasta shells.

Step 4: Secure the lid and ring onto the mason jar. Attach a tag onto the mason jar with the following cooking instructions:

1. Brown 1 pound of ground beef or pork on the stove. Drain the beef.
2. Pour 7 cups and the contents of the jar into the pot and bring to a boil.
3. Add a 15-ounce can of corn and a 15-ounce can of diced tomatoes to the boiling water. Add the browned beef as well.
4. Reduce the heat and let simmer for 25 minutes.

5. Serve the soap with shredded cheese, sour cream and whole tortilla chips.

Multigrain Chicken Soup Mix Gift Jar

Ingredients:

- 1 quart-sized mason jar
- 2/4 cup brown rice, uncooked
- ½ cup barley
- ½ cup yellow split peas
- ½ cup red lentils
- 1 tablespoons dried thyme
- 2 tablespoons dried parsley
- 1 teaspoon dried marjoram
- 1 teaspoon ground ginger
- ½ teaspoon ground black pepper

Directions:

Step 1: Pour the brown rice into the mason jar. Set the jar to the side.

Step 2: Layer the yellow split peas on top of the rice. Layer the red lentils on top of the split peas.

Step 3: Mix the barley, thyme, parsley, marjoram, ground ginger and black pepper together in a bowl. Pour the spice mixture on top of the split peas.

Step 4: Secure the lid on the mason jar. Attach a label to the jar with the following cooking directions:

1. Cut 1 pound of boneless, skinless chicken breasts into bite-sized pieces.
2. Fill a pot with 12 cups of water. Add 2 celery stalks sliced, 2 crushed garlic cloves and 4 large carrots sliced. Add salt and pepper to taste.

3. Add the cut chicken breasts and contents of the mason jar to the pot.
4. Bring the contents of the pot to a boil.
5. Turn the heat down, cover the pot and let simmer for an hour, or until the grains are tender.
6. If necessary, thin the soap with chicken stock or water.

Potato Soup Mix Gift Jar

Ingredients:

- Mason jar
- 2 cups instant potatoes, dry
- 1 ½ cups instant milk powder
- 2 tablespoons instant chicken bullion
- 1 teaspoon powdered garlic
- 1 teaspoon parsley
- ¼ teaspoon thyme
- ¼ teaspoon pepper

Directions:

Step 1: Place all the instant potatoes, instant milk, instant chicken bouillon, garlic, parsley, thyme and pepper in a gallon zip lock bag. Shake the bag for several seconds until the ingredients are well mixed.

Step 2: Pour the contents of the bag into the mason jar. Secure the lid and ring on the jar. On a decorative tag, write the following cooking instructions:

1. Scoop ½ cup of the soup mix into a mug, large cup or bowl.
2. Pour 1 cup of boiling water into the mug, cup or bowl and stir thoroughly until the mixture becomes smooth.

Merry Minestrone Soup Gift Jar

Ingredients:

- 1 quart-sized mason jar
- ½ cup white rice
- ¾ cup split peas
- ¼ cup dried barley
- 1 cup red beans
- ½ cup red lentils
- 1/3 cup beef bouillon
- ¼ cup dried onions, chopped
- 2 tablespoons Italian seasoning
- 1/3 cup pasta

Directions:

Step 1: In the quart-sized mason jar, layer the ingredients in the order listed above.

Step 2: On a tag or label, write the following cooking instructions for the minestrone soup:

1. Brown 1 pound of hamburger meat. Drain and set to the side.
2. Pour 12 cups of water into a large pot. Dump the contents of the mason jar into the water.
3. Slice 2 carrots and 2 celery ribs. Place them in the pot. Dice 1 tomato and add it to the pot.
4. Add the hamburger meat to the pot of water.
5. Cook on medium high, bringing the water to a boil.
6. Reduce heat and let simmer for 45 minutes or until beans are tender.

Healthy Halloween Soup Mix in a Jar

Ingredients:

- Mason jar
- ½ cup small pasta
- 1/3 cup yellow split peas
- 1/3cup red lentils
- 1/3 cup pearl barley
- 2 tablespoons dried onion
- 2 tablespoons dried parsley
- 1 teaspoon dried oregano
- 1 teaspoon dried thyme

Directions:

Step 1: In the mason jar, layer the ingredients one on top of another. Secure the lid and ring on the mason jar.

Step 2: Attach the following cooking instructions onto the jar:

1. Pour soup mix and 8 cups of water into a pot. Place on the stove and bring to a boil.
2. Reduce the heat and let simmer for about 50 minutes or until the peas are tender.
3. If desired, add a can of corn or 1 cup of frozen vegetables.

Treat Jars for Pet Lovers

Dog Biscuit Mason Gift Jar

Ingredients:

- 1 quart-sized mason jar
- Dog bone-shaped cookie cutter
- 2 cups whole wheat flour
- 1 cup parmesan grated cheese
- 2 tablespoons butter, melted
- ¾ cup milk

Directions:

Step 1: Preheat oven to 375-degrees.

Step 2: Mix the whole wheat flour, parmesan, melted butter and milk together in a bowl until well combined.

Step 3: Lightly flour a level surface. Roll the dough out on the floured surface to about ¼-inch thick.

Step 4: Use the bone-shaped cookie cutter to cut cookies out of the dough. Place the cookies on to a cookie sheet.

Step 5: Bake the cookie dough for about 15 minutes. Remove from the oven and let the cookies cool on a wire rake.

Step 6: While the cookies are cooling, cut a dog bone shape from a paper bag. This is the nametag for your gift jar. Write the name of lucky pet who will receive this jar neatly onto the tag. Use a paper hole punch to create a hole in the upper corner of the bone. Thread a decorate ribbon through the hole and secure the tag to the mason jar.

Step 7: Once the cookies have cooled, place them inside the mason jar. Secure the jar closed with the lid and ring.

No Frills Dog Treat Mason Jar Gift

Ingredients:

- 1 quart-sized mason jar
- 1 ½ cups oatmeal
- 2 4-ounce jars or chicken/turkey and pumpkin/sweet potato baby food

Step 1: Preheat the oven to 350-degrees.

Step 2: Pour the oatmeal into a food processor. Grind the up the oatmeal.

Step 3: Dump the baby food into the food processor. Turn the food processor on to combine it with the ground oatmeal.

Step 4: Scoop the dough onto a cookie sheet with a spoon. The size of the treats should depend on the size of the dog. For larger dogs, spoon tablespoon-sized balls onto the cookie sheet, while smaller dogs should have treats about 1 to 1 ½ inches in diameter.

Step 5: Bake the treats in the oven for about 20 to 22 minutes. Remember that smaller-sized treats will require less baking time.

Step 6: Remove the treats from the cookie sheet and let cool completely on a wire rake.

Step 7: Fill the mason jar with the cooled treats. Place the lid on top of the jar and screw down the ring to secure the lid in place. Tell the recipient of the dog treats that they should be stored in the refrigerator.

Tips: Check the baby food ingredients and make sure it doesn't container onion, garlic or other items that can be harmful to dogs.

Dog Cookie Mix Gift Jar

Ingredients:

- 1 quart-sized mason jar
- Dog bone-shaped cookie cutter
- Decorative ribbon
- 1 ¼ cup whole wheat or unbleached flour
- 1 cup oatmeal that has been blended into flour
- ½ cup cornmeal
- 2 teaspoons chicken or beef boullion granules
- 1 teaspoon garlic powder
- 1 cup skim milk powder
- ½ cup parmesan cheese, grated

Directions:

Step 1: Layer the mason jar with the ingredients in the following order: 1 cup flour, oatmeal, cornmeal, boullion granules, garlic powder, skim milk powder, grated parmesan cheese and ¼ cup flour. Make sure to pack each layer down before adding the next.

Step 2: Secure the lid and ring onto the jar. Thread the decorative ribbon through the cookie cutter and tie it around the jar.

Step 3: Attach a decorative label or tag to the mason jar with the following baking instructions:

1. Preheat oven to 250-degrees.
2. Dump the contents of the mason jar into a mixing bowl.

3. Add 1 cup of hot water and 2 large eggs. Stir the ingredients together until well mixed.
4. Lightly flour a cutting board, table or counter. Roll the dough out to about ½-inch thickness.
5. Dip the included bone-shaped cookie cutter into flour and cut the cookies out. Place the cut cookies onto a baking sheet.
6. Bake the dog cookies in the oven for about 90-minutes, or until they become hard and dry. Turning the baking time, turn the baking sheet around at about the 45-minute mark.
7. Let the dog cookies cool completely. Store in a resealable, airtight jar.

Homemade Puppy Treats Gift Jar

Ingredients:

- 1 quart-sized mason jar
- 2 cups whole wheat flour
- 2/3 cup rolled oats
- 2 4-ounce jars baby food (use only baby food that is safe for dogs)

Directions:

Step 1: Preheat oven to 350-degrees. Lightly flour a level surface.

Step 2: Mix together the whole wheat flour, rolled oats and baby food.

Step 3: Roll out the dough on a floured-surface to about ½-inch thick. Use a cookie cutter to cut out the dough. Any shape cookie cutter will do.

Step 4: Place the cutout cookies on a cookie sheet and bake in the oven for around 35-minutes, or until the cookies are hard and dry.

Peanut Carob Clusters Mix Gift Jar

Ingredients:

- 1 pint-sized mason jar
- ¾ cup white rice flour
- ½ cup oats
- ½ cup carob powder
- ½ cup peanuts

Directions:

Step 1: Crush the peanuts and place them to the side.

Step 2: Layer the ingredients in the mason jar as followed: flour, oats, carob powder and peanuts. Make sure to pack each layer down with the back of a spoon before adding the next layer.

Step 3: Place the lid on the mason jar and secure with the ring. Attach a tag of label to the jar with the following baking instructions:

1. Preheat the oven to 350-degrees. Line the baking sheet with parchment paper.
2. Pour the contents of the mason jar into a large mixing bowl. Add 1 cup of milk and stir until well blended.
3. Use a tablespoon to scoop the dough onto the cookie sheet.
4. Bake for about 10 to 15 minutes.

Gingerbread Dog Treat Mix Gift Jar

Ingredients:

- 1 quart-sized mason jar
- 3 cups wheat flour
- ½ teaspoon ground ginger
- 1 teaspoon ground cinnamon
- Dog bone cookie cutter
- Twine or ribbon

Directions:

Step 1: Mix the flour and ginger in a bowl. Pour into the mason jar.

Step 2: Secure the lid and ring onto the jar. Secure the cookie cutter to the mason jar with the twine or ribbon.

Step 3: Attach a label or tag to the jar with the following baking instructions:

1. Preheat oven to 325-degrees. Lightly grease a cookie sheet.
2. Pour the contents of the mason jar into a mixing bowl.
3. Add ¼ cup plus 1 tablespoon of vegetable oil, ½ cup of molasses and ½ cup of water. Stir until all ingredients are well combined.
4. Let the dough rest for 15 minutes. While the dough is resting, lightly flour a level surface.
5. Roll the dough out to about ¼-inch thick. Use the included done bone cookie cutter to cut cookies out of the dough.

6. Transfer the cookies onto the prepared cookie sheet. Bake for about 20 minutes.

Salmon Cat Treat Gift Jar

Ingredients:

- 1 quart-sized mason jar
- Canned salmon in water, 6 or 7 ounces
- ½ cup cornmeal
- ¼ cup non-fat dry milk
- 1 egg
- 1 tablespoon cooking oil
- 2 tablespoons water
- 1 cup whole wheat flour

Directions:

Step 1: Preheat oven to 350-degrees.

Step 2: Combine the salmon, cornmeal, dry milk, egg, cooking oil and water together in a mixing bowl.

Step 3: Add the flour slowly to the mixture, making sure to stir well. The dough is rather heavy so you may need to mix it by hand.

Step 4: Place the dough on a floured surface. Knead the dough a few times. Roll the dough out to about ¼-inch thick.

Step 5: Use a pizza cutter to carefully cut the dough into small cat bite-size pieces.

Step 6: Place the pieces on a cookie sheet. Bake for about 15 minutes. Make sure to watch the treats while baking because they can burn quickly.

Step 7: Let the treats cool completely before placing them in the mason jar. Place the lid and ring to secure the jar closed.

Tune Cat Treat Gift Jar

Ingredients:

- 1 quart-sized mason jar
- 1 four-ounce can tuna in water
- ¼ cup water
- 2 eggs whites, cooked and chopped
- ¼ cup cornmeal
- ½ cup whole wheat flour

Directions:

Step 1: Preheat oven to 350-degrees.

Step 2: Put the egg whites and tuna in a food processor. Pulse the two ingredients until they are chopped fine.

Step 3: Add the water and pulse again to blend. Add the wheat flour and cornmeal. Pulse once again until the mixture is thoroughly blended.

Step 4: Lightly flour a level surface. Roll the dough out on the surface to about ¼-inch thick.

Step 5: Use a pizza cutter to cut the dough into small rectangles that measure about ½-inch by ¼-inch.

Step 6: Place the bite-sized treats on a lightly greased cookie sheet. Bake the treats for about 15 to 20 minutes, or until they become lightly browned.

Step 7: Let the treats cool and place in the mason jar.

Tuna and Catnip Crouton Cat Treats Gift Jar

Ingredients:

- 1 five ounce tuna can, drained
- 1 cup coconut flour
- 1 tablespoon olive oil, extra light
- 1 tablespoon dried catnip
- 1 egg
- 1 to 2 tablespoons water

Directions:

Step 1: Preheat oven to 350-degrees. Line the cookie sheet with parchment paper.

Step 2: Place the tuna, egg, water, coconut flour, catnip and olive oil in a food processor. Blend the ingredients until smooth.

Step 3: Pull small pieces of dough from the food processor and pinch it into a crouton-like shape. Place the crouton

Step 4: Place the crouton treats onto the cookie sheet.

Step 5: Bake the treats for about 12 to 15 minutes, or until the croutons are browned on top and dry.

Step 6: Let the treats cool completely before placing them inside the mason jar.

Tips: These treats should be used within 2 weeks and stored in the fridge.

Spinach and Chicken Cat Treats Gift Jar

Ingredients:

- 1 pint or quart-sized mason jar
- ½ cup skinless and boneless chicken thighs, steamed
- 1 cup spinach leaves, fresh
- 1 cup quick cooking oats
- 1 brown egg
- 1 tablespoon catnip
- ¼ cup flour

Directions:

Step 1: Preheat the oven to 350-degrees.

Step 2: Steam the chicken thighs until they are completely cooked through. Allow the chicken to cool for about 20 minutes.

Step 3: Put the chicken thighs, spinach leaves, catnip, oats and egg in a food processor or blender.

Step 4: Pulse or blend the ingredients until the mixture becomes smooth but a bit chunky. It should have a texture similar to wet sand.

Step 5: Transfer the mixture to a bowl. Add the flour and knead the dough with your hands. Continue kneading until the dough is no longer sticky.

Step 6: Place the dough on a floured surface and roll out to about ½-inch thick.

Step 7: Use a pizza cutter to cut the dough in small shapes. Place the treats on a baking sheet lined with parchment.

Step 8: Bake the treats for 20 minutes before removing them from the oven. Let the treats cool completely before placing them in the mason jar.

Decorating the Treat Jars

If you want give spice up the mason jar but don't have the artistic ability to paint cute puppies and kitties, consider this simple and inexpensive fix:

Step 1: Spray paint the lid and ring of the mason jar with the desired color spray paint. Do the same with a small plastic toy in the shape of either a dog or cat. Let the paint dry completely before continuing.

Step 2: Apply craft glue to the bottom of plastic toy. Press the glue-covered bottom to the top of the lid. Let dry completely before handling.

That's it! You know have an adorably decorative mason jar that makes a great gift when filled with dog or cat treats.

Jars for Bath and Body

Edible Chocolate Body Scrub Gift Jar

Ingredients:

- ½ cup rolled oats
- ½ cup cocoa nibs
- ½ cup kosher salt
- 2 tablespoons cocoa powder, unsweetened
- ½ cup sweet almond oil
- ½ cup jojoba oil
- 2 tablespoons vitamin E oil

Directions:

Step 1: In a blender or food processor, grind the rolled oats until they are powder.

Step 2:Add the cocoa powder, cocoa nibs, kosher salt, jojoba oil, sweet almond oil and vitamin E oil.

Step 3: Pulse the ingredients a few times until they are well incorporated into one another.

Step 4: Spoon the mixture into a quart-sized mason jar. Decorate the jar by tying a decorative ribbon or twine around it.

Step 5: Attach a label or tag to the jar that reads, "Massage the edible chocolate body scrub into your skin. Rinse with warm water."

Honey and Grits Exfoliating Body Scrub Gift Jar

Ingredients:

- 1 vitamin E capsule

- ½ cup honey, organic

- ¼ cup grits

- 1 teaspoon sweet almond oil

Directions:

Step 1: Dump the grits into a mixing bowl. Add the honey and sweet almond oil.

Step 2: With a wooden spoon, mix the three ingredients together until well blended.

Step 3: Pierce the vitamin E capsule with a needle or knife. Dump the contents of the capsule into the mixture. Stir once again with the wooden spoon.

Step 4: Scoop the body scrub into a mason jar. Attach a label to the jar with the following instructions:

1. Use your fingers to scoop a bit of the body scrub out of the jar.

2. Rub the scrub into damp skin using a gentle circular motion.

3. Rinse the scrub off with warm water.

4. Store unused scrub in the fridge.

Miscellaneous Gift Jar Crafts

Hot Coco for Adults Gift Jar

Ingredients:

- Mason jars
- Hot chocolate mix
- Mini marshmallows
- Bailey alcohol, individual bottles
- Twin

Directions:

Step 1: Fill the mason jar about ½ full with hot chocolate.

Step 2: Fill the remaining space with mini marshmallows.

Step 3: Secure the lid and ring on the mason jar.

Step 4: Attach the small bottle of Bailey's to the jar with twin.

Step 5: Give the gift jar to adults!

White Hot Chocolate Mix Gift Jar

Ingredients:

- Mason jar
- 1 cup white chocolate chips
- 1 package instant white chocolate pudding, 3.3-ounce
- 1 cup instant dry milk

Directions:

Step 1: Freeze the white chocolate chips for about an hour. Place the frozen chips into a blender and grind them until they become a powder.

Step 2: Mix the ground-up white chocolate chips, instant white chocolate pudding and instant dry milk together.

Step 3: Pour the mixture into the mason jar. Secure the lid and ring on the jar.

Step4: Attach a label to the jar with the following information: Use 3 teaspoons of the mix for every cup of hot water. Stir thoroughly and enjoy on a cold day!

Potpourri and Lights Gift Jar

Materials:

- 1 quart-sized mason jar
- 1 bag of potpourri, small
- 1 strand of 30-count lights, white or colored
- 1 rubber band
- 1 doily
- 1 piece of ribbon

Directions:

Step 1: Stuff the potpourri and lights into the mason jar, making sure to leave the plug-in portion of the light cord out of the jar.

Step 2: Place the doily over the top of the mason jar. Use your hand to smooth the doily down around the lip of the jar and secure it in place with a rubber band.

Step 3: Tie the ribbon around the rubber band. The ribbon adds an additional decorative touch to the jar while hiding the ugly rubber band.

Step 4: When the lights are plugged in they should begin to produce heat. This heat will cause the potpourri to release its smell.

Gingerbread House Kit Gift Jar

Materials:

- 1 quart-sized mason jar
- 6 graham cracker squares
- Small candies, such as mini M&Ms, Reese's Pieces, Starbursts
- Royal icing
- Ziplock bags
- Decorative ribbon
- Gift tag

Directions:

Step 1: Spoon about ½ cup of royal icing into the corner of the ziplock bag.

Step 2: Place the royal icing-filled bag on the bottom of the jar.

Step 3: Insert the graham cracker squares into the mason jar.

Step 4: Pour the small candies into the jar. Continuing adding the candies until the jar is filled.

Step 5: Secure the lid and ring onto the jar. Write the desired message on the tag. Feed the ribbon through the hole in the tag. Tie the ribbon around the mason jar.

Homemade Playdough Mix Gift Jar

Materials:

- 1 quart-sized mason jar
- 1 cup all-purpose flour
- ½ cup salt
- 2 teaspoons cream of tartar
- Twine
- Cookie cutter (optional)

Directions:

Step 1: Mix the flour, cream of tartar and salt together in a mixing bowl.

Step 2: Transfer the mixture into the mason jar. Secure the lid and ring on the jar.

Step 3: Create a label with the following instructions on it:

1. Dump the mix into a pot. Add 1 cup of water and 1 tablespoons of vegetable oil.
2. Place the pot on the stove and cook on medium while stirring continuously.
3. When the mixture begins to thicken, add a few drops of food coloring. Continue stirring.
4. Once thickened, remove the mixture from heat and dump onto a piece of parchment paper to cool.
5. The playdough is ready to use once cooled! When not in use, store in the fridge.

Step 4: Tie a cute cookie cutter to the mason jar with a bit of twin.

Step 5: Give the gift jar to the lucky recipient.

Monster Kit Gift Jar

Materials:

- Quart-sized mason jar
- PomPoms, various sizes
- Pipe cleaners
- Popsicle sticks
- Small bottle of craft glue
- Google eyes
- Small baggie
- Various accessories (optional)

Directions:

Step 1: Place the google eyes in a small baggie. Set aside for the moment.

Step 2: Set the craft glue in the mason jar. Position the pipe cleaners and popsicle sticks around the glue. Push the PomPoms and other accessories into the jar. Try to pack the jar as tight as possible.

Step 3: Lay the google eye-filled baggie on top of the items. Secure the lid and ring on the jar.

Step 4: Attach a cute label to the jar that reads: "Monster Kit".

Christmas Cocoa Mix Gift Jar

Ingredients:

- 1 quart-sized mason jar
- Instant hot chocolate mix
- Mini marshmallows
- Chocolate chips
- Starlight mints, unwrapped

Directions:

Step 1: Pour 2 cups of hot chocolate mix into the bottom of the jar.

Step 2: Place a layer of about 1 cup of mini marshmallows on top of the mix, followed by ½ cup of chocolate chips.

Step 3: Add about 20 unwrapped starlight mints on top of the chocolate chips.

Step4: Attach the lid and ring to the jar. Place a label on the jar that reads:

1. Mix 2 tablespoons of the mix with 1 cup of hot milk.
2. Stir in the chocolate chips, mini marshmallows and/or mints.
3. Enjoy!

Whole Wheat Chocolate Chip Pancake Mix Gift Jar

Ingredients:

- Mason jar
- 3 ½ cups old-fashioned oats
- 1 cup all-purpose unbleached flour
- 4 cups white whole wheat flour
- 3 tablespoons sugar
- 3 tablespoons baking powder
- 1 tablespoon baking soda
- 1 tablespoon salt
- 1 cup vegetable oil
- 1 cup mini chocolate chips

Directions:

Step 1: Grind the oats up into a food processor. Avoid grinding them up too much. You don't want them to be a powder.

Step 2: Place the oats in a mixing bowl. Add the flours, baking powder, baking soda, salt and sugar. Mix thoroughly until the ingredients are well incorporated.

Step 3: Slowly drizzle the oil over the dry ingredients and mix again. Fold in the chocolate chips.

Step 4: Transfer the mixture into the mason jar. Secure the lid and ring on the mason jar.

Step 5: Attach a label or tag to the mason jar with the following cooking directions:

1. Add 1 cup of the pancake mix to a bowl.

2. Add 1 large egg and 1 cup of buttermilk.
3. Whisk all the ingredients together.
4. Let the batter sit for 20 minutes.
5. While the batter is resting, grease a griddle on heat on medium heat.
6. Pour ¼ cup of the batter on the heated griddle and cook until bubbles begin to form in the batter.
7. Flip the pancake over and cook on the other side.
8. Store unused pancake mix in the fridge for up to 2 weeks.

Dill Beer Bread Mix Gift Jar

Ingredients:

- Quart-sized mason jar
- 2 ¾ cups all-purpose flour
- 1 tablespoon sugar
- 2 teaspoons baking powder
- 1 teaspoon salt
- 1 tablespoon dill weed, dried

Directions:

Step 1: Mix the flour, sugar, baking powder, salt and dried dill weed together in a bowl.

Step 2: Pour the dill beer bread mix into the mason jar. Secure the lid and ring on the jar.

Step 3: Attach a label or tag with the following cooking instructions:

1. Preheat oven to 375-degrees
2. Grease a 9-inch by 5-inch loaf pan.
3. Pour the contents of the mason jar into a mixing bowl.
4. Add 12-ounces of beer into the bowl and mix thoroughly.
5. Pour the batter into the loaf pan and bake for about 40 minutes, or when a toothpick inserted into the bread comes out clean.
6. Let the bread cool for about 15 minutes.
7. Brush the top of the bread with melted butter.

Chapter 4 – Mason Jar Home Decor: Turn Those Old Mason Jars into a Useful Part of your Home

Storage and Organizing: Declutter your Home with the Help of Mason Jars

Mason Jar Craft Storage

Materials Needed:

- Wire basket
- Mason jars
- Chalkboard spray paint
- Chalk pen

Directions:

Step 1: Spray paint the top of the lids with the chalkboard paint. Let dry for several hours before continuing.

Step 2: After the paint has dried, neatly write the on the painted lids what will be stored in the mason jar.

Step 3: Place the mason jars in the wire basket. Fill them with the desired craft items and secure closed with the painted lid and ring.

Mason Jar Bathroom Storage

Materials

- 2'x7" wooden board
- Mason Jars
- Wood stain or paint
- Picture hanging kit
- Hose clamps
- Drill and screws
- Screwdriver

Step 1: Stain or paint the wooded board the desired color. Let dry completely before continuing.

Step 2: Determine where you want the mason jars to hang from the wooden board. Make a mark on the wooden board with a pencil in the middle of the area where the each mason jar will go.

Step 3: Position the middle of the clamp over the mark you made in Step 2. Secure the clamp onto the board with screws. Repeat the process on the remaining marks.

Step 4: Use the picture hanging kit to hang the wooden board in the desired location.

Step 5: Insert the mason jar into the middle of the hose clamp. Use a screwdriver to secure the clamp closed and keep the mason jar in place.

Step 6: Fill the mason jars with the desired items.

Playroom Mason Jar Storage

Materials:

- Small plastic toys
- Spray paint
- Mason jars
- Craft glue

Directions:

Step 1: Spray paint small plastic toys, mason jar lids and mason jar rings with colorful spray paint. Let the paint dry completely.

Step 2: Apply craft glue on the bottom of the plastic toys. Press the toys against the top of the lid. Make sure that, if you are using different colors of spray paint, you match the painted toys with the same color of painted lid.

Step 3: Let the glue dry completely before continuing.

Step 4: Fill the jars with the desired items – such as crayons, markers and craft supplies – and secure the rings and lid onto the jars.

Magnetic Mason Jar Spice Rack

Materials:

- Sheet of stainless steel
- Neodymium magnets
- Craft glue
- Quilted mason jars, 4-ounces
- Jar caps, one-piece
- Labels

Directions:

Step 1: Mount the sheet of stainless steel to the desired area where you will keep the spice rake.

Step 2: Write the name of the spices on the labels. Attach the labels to the jars.

Step 3: Glue the magnets onto the middle top of the jar's cap. Let the glue dry.

Step 4: Pour the spices into the correct container. Secure the jar closed with the lid. The mason jars will now attach to the stainless steel sheet via the magnet on the lid.

Let There Be Light: Make your Own Lighting with Mason Jars

Mason Jar Oil Lamp

Materials:

- Mason jar
- Cotton wick
- Lamp oil
- Nail

Directions:

Step 1: Create a hole in the top of the mason jar lid with a nail. The hole needs to be large enough to pull the wick through.

Step 2: Pull the cotton wick through the hole. You need about ¼-inch of the wick sticking out of the top of the lid.

Step 3: Carefully fill the mason jar about 2/3 full with lamp oil.

Step 4: Secure the lid and ring onto the mason jar. When ready to use, light the wick.

Tips: A cotton shoelace works well as an alternative to a cotton wick.

Mason Jar Floating Candles Centerpieces

Materials:

- Mason jars
- Decorative rocks or marbles
- Floating candles
- Decorative ribbon or twin

Directions:

Step 1: Line the bottom of the mason jar with decorative rocks or marbles.

Step 2: Fill the mason jars a little less then ¾ full of water.

Step 3: Tie a decorative ribbon or twin around the top of the mason jar.

Step 4: Carefully sit a floating candle into the water-filled mason jar. Light when ready to use.

Mason Jar Pendant Light

Materials:

- Mason jar
- Pendant light cords
- Light bulbs
- Drill and drill bit

Directions:

Step 1: Drill a hole into the lid of the mason jar large enough so the light cord pulls easily through.

Step 2: Feed the pendant light cord through the hole and attach the light bulb. Secure the lid and ring onto the mason jar. The tension in the light cord will keep the bulb in place.

Step 3: Have a professional (or someone who has installed pendant lighting in the past) install the pendant light.

Mason Jar Lamp

Materials:

- Mason jar
- Light kit

Step 1: Drill a hole in the mason jar lid.

Step 2: Insert the "stopper" into the hole. The "stoppers" are included in the light kit.

Step 3: Follow the instructions included in the light kit. These instructions vary depending on each brand of light kit and you must follow them to properly create the mason jar lamp.

<u>Mason Jar Chandelier</u>

Materials:

- 12 mason jars
- Medium-density fiberboard or inexpensive pine
- Drill
- Paint
- 12 keyless sockets
- Lamp cord
- Wire cutters
- Light bulbs that will fit inside the mason jars and fit the sockets
- Wire nuts

Directions:

Step 1: Determine the size you want the ceiling plate. This is where the wires and lights will attach. Cut the fiberboard or pine to fit the desired size.

Step 2: Decide where you want the lights and wires to go. Drill holes in the fiberboard or pine in the appropriate location.

Step 3: Attach small pieces of the pine or fiberboard to all sides of the ceiling plate. This creates a shallow box that you will attach to the ceiling.

Step 4: Paint the entire ceiling plate. Let dry before continuing.

Step 5: For each mason jar, cut the lamp cord to the desired length. Keep in mind that if you cut each lamp cord the same length then the mason jars will clank together when hanging. To prevent this, cut each cord a different length.

Step 6: Use the drill to create a hole in the middle of the mason jar lids. Create two holes a bit smaller on each side of the larger middle hole. These smaller holes will help prevent the mason jar from overheating.

Step 7: Secure one end of the lamp cord to the keyless socket. Screw the light bulb in place. Carefully slide the mason jar lid on top. The lid should fit snugly against the socket.

Step 8: Thread the lamp cord through the holes created in the ceiling plate. Secure them in place with a knot.

Step 9: Strip the end of the wire cord and attach them to a wire nut.

Step 10. Screw the ceiling plate box into the ceiling. Carefully secure the mason jars to the lids.

Step 11: An electrician should be consulted to properly install the light fixture.

Vintage Praire-Style Mason Jar Rope Light

Materials:

- Mason jar
- Lamp cord kit
- Jute rope
- Jute twine
- Hot glue
- White craft glue
- Scissor
- Drill with drill bits

Directions:

Step 1: Cut the jute rope to the desired length.

Step 2: Place white craft glue to the upper portion of the light bulb socket. Wrap the jute twine around the glue-covered part of the socket.

Step 3: Carefully pull three pieces of the jute rope apart. Retwine the jute rope around the lamp cord. Use the hot glue to secure the rope around the cord.

Step 4: Wrap the jute twine tightly around the ending and beginning portion of the rope. Secure the twine in place with hot glue.

Step 5: Cut a hole big enough for the light socket to pass through in the mason jar lid. Carefully push the socket through the lid to the stopper where the jute twin begins.

Step 6: Carefully create two smaller vent holes on each side of the larger hole.

Step 7: Carefully twist the female part of the light socket up to the mason jar lid. This secures the jar/lid to the light cord.

Mason Jar Light

Materials:

- 5 large-mouth mason jars
- Burlap ribbon
- Grapevine wire
- 100 white lights
- Swivel hooks

Directions:

Step 1: Make a small ring in the grapevine by twisting the grapevine around a pencil. Wrap the vine around the mouth of the mason jar and twist. Take the grapevine wire and secure it to the ring you made. You have made the grapevine hanger. Place the mason jar ring on the jar to help keep the grapevine wire in place.

Step 2: Hang the mason jars where you like. Use the burlap ribbon if you want to hang the jars lower than others.

Step 3: Carefully tuck the white lights into the mason jars. Play around with the lights until you achieve the desired look.

Simple Mason Jar Candle Holders or Centerpieces

Ingredients:

- Mason jars
- Candles
- Decorative stones or sand

Directions:

Step 1: Fill the mason jar with the decorative stones or sand. The amount used will vary depending on the size of the candle, how far you want it sticking above the jar and your specific desires.

Step 2: Place the candle into the middle of the jar. Move the sand or stones around so it helps stabilize the candle.

Step 3: Place the jars in the desired location. Light the candles when ready to use.

Fillers for Mason Jar Candle Holders

Marbles, sand, pebbles and sea glass are the four most common fillers for mason jar candle holders. And while they are all well and good, sometimes you want something a bit different. This is when you need to think outside the box. In fact, just about anything you can stuff into the mason jar will work as a filler.

If you're looking for inexpensive filler, simply take a walk down the bean and grain aisle of your local department store. Black eyed peas, pearl barley, quinoa and white beans are a few filler options for your mason jar candle holders. Any dehydrated bean, nut, rice or grain can be turned into a filler! You can also mix and match them for a colorful creation. Popcorn kernels also make a fun filler for any movie or Hollywood-themed part.

To use these fillers, simply pour them into the mason jar so that the jar is about a quart or third full. Keep in mind, however, that you can add as much or as little of the filler as you like. It's all about making a candle holder that fits your desires and taste. Set the candle in the middle and press down slightly. Ta da! All done!

Mason Jar Luminaries

Materials:

- Mason jar
- Decorative glass gems
- Hot glue gun and glue sticks
- Tea candles

Directions:

Step 1: Start at the top of the mason jar and hot glue the gems to the exterior of the jar. You want the gems to cover the entire mason jar exterior.

Step 2: Let the glue dry before placing the tea candle in the middle of the jar and lighting.

Mason Jar Lamp

Materials:

- 25 watt lightbulb
- Push-thru side out socket
- 1-inch threaded rod
- Check ring with 3/8-inch diameter
- 1-inch diameter rubber washer
- 1 quart-sized mason jar
- Clip on lamp shade
- Decorative rocks, stones or pebbles
- Drill
- 3/8-inch drill bit

Directions:

Step 1: With the drill and drill bit, drill a hole directly into the center of the mason jar lid.

Step 2: Feed the 1-inch threaded rod through the hole you just created in the lid. The amount of threaded rod you leave sticking above the lid will depend on how high you want the light bulb to be from the base of the lamp.

Step 3: Screw the push-thru socket through the top part of the lid and onto the 1-inch threaded rod.

Step 4: Set the rubber washer on the rod at the underside portion of the lid. Screw the check ring on. Remember to ensure the ring is tightened to make sure everything stays in place.

Step 5: Place the desired amount of decorative rocks, stones or pebbles into the mason jar.

Step 6: Screw the lid on the mason jar. The socket should be pointing upward.

Step 7: Screw the light bulb into the socket and attach the lampshade on the mason jar.

Doily Lumineers

Materials:

- Mason jar
- Fabric doily
- Burlap
- Adhesive spray
- Buttons, ribbon and/or twine
- Tealight candle

Directions:

Step 1: Spray the doily with adhesive spray and immediately lay on top of the mason jar.

Step 2: Make sure the doily covers the entire jar. Furthermore, you want the doily to be smooth and not bunched up anywhere on the jar.

Step 3: Spray the rim of the jar carefully with adhesive. Press the burlap against and around the rim.

Step 4: Decorate the jar with buttons, ribbon and/or twin. For a more minimal look, simply skip this step.

Step 5: Place a candle in the middle of the jar. Place the jar in the desired location. Light when ready to use.

Vases and Picture Frames: Decorate your Home with Upcycled Mason Jars

Painted Mason Jar Vases

Ingredients:

- Mason jars
- Acrylic craft paint
- Newspaper
- Cardboard
- Plastic or paper cups that can fit inside the mason jars (optional)

Directions:

Step 1: Cover your work area with newspaper. This will protect the surface from paint splatters, drips or splashes.

Step 2: Squirt a liberal amount of the desired color of acrylic craft paint into the bottom of the mason jar. About ½-inch of paint should be good enough.

Step 3: Turn the jar mostly upside down, twirling it slowly. You want to keep moving the jar so that the paint covers the entire inside of the mason jar. Remember to keep the jar over the newspaper.

Step 4: Once the entire inside of the jar is covered, turn the jar upside on a piece of cardboard. Let the excessive paint dripping out of the jar and onto the cardboard. Move the jars ever 10 to 15 minutes. This will allow the excess paint to escape.

Step 5: Once all or at least most of the excess paint has been removed, turn the jars right side up and let dry for several hours.

Step 6: If you are going to use the vases to hold live flowers, place a plastic or paper cup inside the jar and fill that up with water only. Acrylic paint is water-based and pouring water directly into the painted jar will wash away the paint. This step can be skipped if the vases will not hold live flowers.

Designer Mason Jar Decorative Vase

Materials:

- Mason jar
- Fabric marker
- Hot glue gun and hot glue sticks
- Matte spray paint

Directions:

Step 1: Decide on what design you want on the mason jar. For example, you can write the word love in cursive writing or draw a few hearts.

Step 2: Once you have determined what and where your design will go, use the fabric marker to achieve the look.

Step 3: Trace the design that you made on the mason jar with the hot glue. Let the glue dry completely before continuing.

Step 4: Shake the matte spray paint can for several seconds before removing the lid. Hold the can about 6 to 10 inches away from the mason jar and spray the entire exterior of the jar using a steady back-and-forth motion.

Step 5: Let the spray paint dry for several hours before handling.

Vintage Mason Jar Photo Frame

Materials:

- Mason jar
- Black and white photograph
- Olive oil

Directions:

Step 1: Place the photograph in the mason jar. Position it so the front of the photo is seen from the front of the jar.

Step 2: Fill the jar with olive oil.

Step 3: Secure the jar closed with the lid and ring.

Mason Jar Picture Frame Vase

Materials:

- Mason jar
- Interior satin paint
- Paint brush
- Photograph
- Painter's Tape
- Clear spray paint

Directions:

Step 1: Create the picture frame window on the mason jar by covering the area you want saved as the "window" with painter's tape.

Step 2: Use the paint brush to paint the entire mason jar with the desired color of satin paint.

Step 3: Once the jar is completely painted, immediately remove the painter's tape.

Step 4: Spray the clear spray paint over the entire exterior of the mason jar. This will help seal the satin paint.

Step 5: Let the clear spray paint dry completely before continuing.

Step 6: Place a small piece of painter's tape on all four edges of the photograph. The sticky part of the tape should be facing up so you can attach the photograph to the inside of the mason jar.

Step 7: Place the photograph inside the mason jar and position it so it can be seen through the picture frame window. Press the tape along the edges of the picture to the inside of the jar to secure the picture in place.

Tips: You can easily change the picture when desired by carefully pulling the picture and tape off the inside of the jar and replacing it with the desired photograph.

Inside Out Painted Mason Jar Vases

Materials:

- Mason jars
- Spray paint
- Painter's tape
- Ziplock baggies, large

Directions:

Step 1: Cover the exterior of the mason jars by wrapping them with the ziplock baggies. Secure the baggie in place with painter's tape. Some tape wrapped around the top of the jar is usually sufficient.

Step 2: Carefully spray the inside of the mason jar with the spray paint. You may have to apply 2 coats of paint to the inside. Just make sure to let the paint dry completely between each coat.

Step 3: Once the paint is completely dry, unwrap the baggies. The mason jar vases are now ready to use.

Glitter Dipped Mason Jar Vases

Materials:

- Mason jars
- ModPodge
- Sponge brush
- Glitter
- Painter's Tape

Version 1 Directions:

Step 1: Use the sponge brush to paint a thin coat of ModPodge on the inside of the mason jar. Make sure to cover the interior walls of the jar with the ModPodge.

Step 2: Dump a liberal amount of glitter into the mason jar.

Step 3: Roll the jar around in your hands so that the glitter evenly covers the inside of the jar. The glitter should stick to the ModPodge.

Step 4: Let the ModPodge dry for several hours.

Step 5: Place a piece of paper on a flat surface. Turn the mason jar over to remove any excess glitter inside. Use the paper to funnel the excess glitter back into its container.

Version 2 Directions:

Step 1: Use the painter's tape to make off the exterior area of the mason jar where you don't want glitter to be.

Step 2: Paint the ModPodge onto the exterior of the area not covered with painter's tape.

Step 3: Sprinkle the glitter over the ModPodge covered area. To help with clean up, hold the jar over a piece of paper when sprinkling the glitter.

Step 4: Let the ModPodge dry for several hours. While holding the jar above a piece of paper, gently tap the jar to remove any excess glitter.

Sea Glass Mason Jar Vases

Materials:

- ModPodge, matte finish
- Food coloring
- Water
- Empty containers for mixing
- Plastic silverware for mixing
- Paintbrushes
- Sponge paintbrushes

Version 1 Directions:

Step 1: Add a bit of ModPodge to an empty container.

Step 2: Add the food coloring and water, one drop at a time and mixing after each drop, to the ModPodge until you achieve the desired color.

Step 3: Pour the mixture into the mason jar. Swirl the jar around until the inside is completely coated with the mixture.

Step 4: Lay newspaper down on a flat surface. Turn the mason jar upside down to allow for the excess mixture to drain out.

Step 5: After 10 to 15 minutes, turn the mason jar right side up and let air dry completely.

Version 2 Directions:

Step 1: Add a bit of ModPodge to an empty container.

Step 2: Add the food coloring and water, one drop at a time and mixing after each drop, to the ModPodge until you achieve the desired color.

Step 3: With a sponge paintbrush, paint the exterior of the mason jar with the mixture. You may have to apply more than one coat to get the desired results.

Step 4: Let the jar dry completely before using.

Mason Jar Frames

Materials:

- Mason jars
- Photos
- Scissors or x-acto knife
- Ruler
- Pencil

Directions:

Step 1: Use the ruler to measure how tall the jar is. The photo that will be going into the jar will need to be no taller than this height. If need, trim the photo with scissors or an x-acto knife.

Step 2: Carefully roll the photo up just enough so you can slide it into the mason jar. Make sure that when you roll it the photo is right-side-up when the mason jar is turned upside-down.

Step 3: Use the eraser end of a pencil or your fingers to poke and prod the photo into place.

Step 4: Turn the mason jar upside and place in the desired location to show off your beloved photos.

Everything But the Kitchen Sink: Mason Jar Crafts for the Kitchen

Balloon Dipped Mason Jar Cups

Materials:

- Mason jars
- Balloons in various colors
- Scissors

Directions:

Step 1: Fold the balloon longwise in half.

Step 2: With the scissors, snip a quarter inch or so off the top of the balloon.

Step 3: Cut the skinny part of the balloon – the area where you place your mouth to blow the balloon up – off.

Step 4: Pull the cut balloon over the bottom of the mason jar. Continue pulling up the sides of the jar.

There you have it. Balloon dipped mason jar cups. This project is so easy and inexpensive that you can change the balloons to match holidays, seasons and special occasions.

Mason Jar Sippy Cup

Materials:

- Mason jar
- Drill with drill bit
- Nail file
- Rubber grommet (optional)
- Straw

Directions:

Step 1: Attach the lid and ring to the mason jar.

Step 2: Create a hole in the lid with the drill. The hole should be in the center or to the side.

Step 3: Use the nail file to sand down any sharp places in the hole you just created.

Step 4: Squeeze and push the rubber grommet into the hole. This will create a seal. You can skip this step if desired.

Step 5: Make sure to wash the mason jar thorough before using. There will be tiny metal pieces inside the jar from where you drilled the hole in the lid.

Step 6: Place the straw in the hole and enjoy!

Mason Jar Cupcake Liner Storage

Mason jars make a fun way to store cupcake liner. Not only does it keep the cupcake liners from becoming dusty and covered in debris, but the clear glass also provides a bit of a decorative look to your kitchen shelf. To use, simply place the cupcake liners on top of one another and set inside the mason jar. Secure the lid and ring on the jar to keep the cupcake liners from becoming dirty.

Mason Jar Toothpick Dispenser

Materials:

- Jelly mason jar
- Hammer
- Nail
- Toothpicks

Directions:

Step 1: Carefully hammer the nail into the lid of the jelly mason jar.

Step 2: Continue in this manner until you have a lid with an abundance of holes in the top.

Step 3: Fill the jar with toothpicks. Secure the lid in place.

Step 4: When ready to use, simply turn the jar upside down and shake to remove a toothpick.

Tip: If you want to spruce up the look of the jar, you can tie a decorate bow around the rim of it or hand paint a design on the exterior of the jar.

Mason Jar Candy Dish Pedestals

Materials:

- Mason jars
- Glass candlesticks
- e-6000 glue
- Spray paint in the desired color

Directions:

Step 1: Spray the mason jar lids, rings and candlesticks with the spray paint. You should only use spray paint outdoors or in a well-ventilated area. You may have to apply more than one coat of spray paint to achieve the desired look. If this is the case, let the spray paint dry completely between coats.

Step 2: Once all the paint is dried, carefully apply the e-6000 glue to the bottom of the mason jar. Wait 30 seconds and then press the candlestick against the glue-covered bottom. Make sure the candlestick is centered!

Step 3: Let the glue dry for at least 24 hours.

Step 4: Place the candy dish pedestals in the desired location, fill with candy and attach the lid and rings in place.

Tip: For easier opening and closing of the jars, glue the mason jar lids to the rings to make one piece instead of two separate pieces.

The Great Outdoors: Mason Jar Crafts for your Garden, Patio and Porch

Mason Jar Outdoor String Lights

Materials:

- Half pint-sized mason jars
- 1/16-inch ferrules and stop
- 1/16-inch galvanized cable, enough length to string the area
- Tealight candles
- Nail
- Hammer

Directions:

Step 1: Use the nail and hammer to create matching holes on the mason jar ring. The holes should be across from one another. Repeat the process for all the mason jar rings.

Step 2: Attach the ferrule on one end of the galvanized cable. Feed the cable through one of the holes created in Step1.

Step 3Make a loop with the cable and insert its end in the other hole. Flatten the ferrule by hammering it with the hammer. This will cause it to clamp shut.

Step 4: Feed the open end of the galvanized cable through every lid. A good general rule of thumb is to have 1 lid for every foot of cable.

Step 5: Once you have all the lids attached, create a loop at the end of the cable and close like you did in Step 3.

Step 6: Move the lids along the cable until you position them in the desired area. Hand the cable by the loops.

Step 7: Place a tea light candle inside each mason jar. Light the candles. Screw the mason jar onto rings. Once the rings are secure to the jar, the jars won't slide around.

Simple Hanging Mason Jar Lanterns

Materials:

- Mason jars
- Twine
- Tealight candles
- Scissors

Directions:

Step 1: Tie a piece of twine around the mason jar rim.

Step 2: Cut 3 pieces of the twin measuring about 24 inches long. Tie two of the pieces of time together in the middle. Tie the third piece of twin on. You should know have a piece of twin that has a knot in the middle and six strands branching out from this knot. It should have a formation similar to a spider.

Step 3: Place the twin down on a level surface. Gently stretch the six strands out.

Step 4: Place the mason jar on top of the twin, centering it on the knot.

Step 5: Stretch each strand up along the side of the jar. Feed each strand through the twin that you attached to the rim of the jar in Step 1. Try to get each strand evenly around the mason jar so you have six twin stripes running down the side of the jar.

Step 6: After all six strands have been fed through the twin at the rim of the mason jar, tie a tight knot at the top. Wrap a second piece of twin around the rim of the mason jar and secure with a knot.

Step 7: Place a candle in the middle of the jar and hang from a tree branch, porch, patio or other outdoor location. Light the candle when ready to use.

Mason Jar Herb Garden

Materials:

- Mason jars
- Old wooden board
- Triangle ring hangers
- Pipe clamps
- Picture hanger
- Stainless hanging wire
- Chalkboard paint
- Chalk
- Brush
- Hammer
- Nails
- Screwdriver
- Potting soil
- Seedlings in the desired herbs

Directions:

Step 1: Decide where you want the mason jars to hang on the wooden board. Remember that the jars should be spaced evenly. When you have the desired placement, make a mark on the board with a pencil where each jar will go.

Step 2: Paint a rectangle on the wooden board with chalkboard paint. These rectangles should be positioned directly underneath where the mason jar will hang. This will be where you write the name of the herb in chalk. Using chalkboard paint gives you the ability to easy change the name if you replace the herbs.

Step 3: Attach the pipe clamp to the wooden board. This can be done by hammering nails through the holes located on the clamp. These clamps should be positioned on the marks you made in Step 1.

Step 4: Turn the board over and nail the triangle ring hangers in place. Tie the hanging wire to the ring hangers. This wire is how you will hang the herb garden up.

Step 5: Pour potting soil in the mason jars. Plant the seedlings in the soil. If you are worried about drainage. Add a 1-inch layer of pebbles to the bottom of the jar before adding the soil.

Step 6: Insert the mason jars carefully into the pipe clamps attached to the wooden board. Secure the clamps tight with a screwdriver.

Step 7: Hang the herb garden in the desired location. Most herbs require 6 to 8 hours of sun for proper growth so you should keep this in mind when choosing the spot for the herbs.

Tip: If you don't want to go through the hassle of attaching the mason jars to a decorative wooden board, simply skip those steps and instead set the mason jar herb garden on your porch or in your kitchen.

Mason Jar Fairy Garden

Materials:

- Mason jar
- Pebbles
- Activated charcoal
- Potting soil
- Moss
- Small toys (optional)
- Air-dry clay
- White and red paint
- Toothpick
- Paintbrush

Directions:

Step 1: Make the toadstools for the fairy garden by shaping the clay into two pieces, the stem and the top of the toadstool. Use the toothpick to connect the stem and top together. Follow the drying instructions on the clay package. Once the toadstool is dry, paint it red with white spots. Let the paint dry completely.

Step 2: Layer the pebbles on the bottom of the jar. Add a layer of charcoal.

Step 3: Layer the potting soil next, then followed by the moss.

Step 4: Place the toadstool, tiny pebbles and any small toys you think a fairy would like inside the mason jar.

Step 5: Miss the inside of the mason jar with water. Attach the lid and ring. Place the fairy garden in an area where it won't receive direct sunlight.

DIY Soil Test in a Mason Jar

Materials:

- Mason jar
- Soil from your garden
- Water

Directions:

Step 1: Fill the mason jar about half way full with soil from your garden. If you want an overall test of the soil, take soil from various areas of your yard. If, however, you just want the specific information for a certain area, take soil only from that location.

Step 2: Pour water into the jar. You want the water to come almost to the top of the jar while still leaving room for shaking.

Step 3: Secure the lid on the jar. Shake the mason jar vigorously for several minutes.

Step 4: After shaking, place the mason jar on a level surface in an area where it won't be disturbed. Let the particles settle for several hours. How the separate and settle – into sand, silt and clay layers – will determine the type of soil you have.

Reading the Results:

- The heavier particles – like rocks and sand – will settle to the bottom.
- Silt particles will settle next.
- Clay particles will settle on top of the silt.
- Floating on the water surface will be organic matter.

The ideal soil is called loam and is a good balance of clay, silt and sand. Generally an combination of 40-percent sand, 40-percent silt and 20-percent clay is best.

Sandy loam soil will have a combination of about 65-percent sand, 20-percent silt and 15-percent clay.

Silty loam soil will have a combination of about 65-percent silt, 20-percent sand and 15-percent clay.

Silty clay loam will have a general combination of 60-percent silt, 30-percent clay and 10-percent sand.

If you have a soil combination that is less then desirable, you can amend it by incorporating organic materials into it. Manure, compost and mulch are three common amendments that can be added to poor soil.

Chapter 5 – For the Kids: Mason Jar Crafts you can make with Children

Mason Jar Snow Globe

Materials:

- Mason jar
- Distilled water
- Glitter
- Liquid glycerin
- Figurine(s), such as a plastic toy or tree from a Christmas village
- Crazy glue

Directions:

Step 1: Use the crazy glue to carefully attach the figurine(s) to the mason jar lid. You want to make sure you glue them to the inside portion of the lid, not the outside.

Step 2: Let the glue dry for 12 to 24 hours.

Step 3: Fill the mason jar almost to the top with distilled water.

Step 4: Add a little dash of liquid glycerin to the water. The glycerin will make the glitter fall more slowly.

Step 5: Add the glitter. The amount of glitter used really only depends on how you want the snow globe to look.

Step 6: Screw the lid onto the mason jar. Turn the jar upside, give it a little shake and watch the "snow" fall!

Glow Jar

Materials:

- Mason jar
- Glow-in-the-dark paint
- Paintbrush

Directions:

Step 1: Use the paintbrush to mix the glow-in-the-dark paint gently.

Step 2: With the paint on the end of the brush, make small dots on the inside of the mason jar.

Step 3: Continue making dots all over the inside of the jar until you achieve the desired look.

Step 4: Let the paint dry completely. When ready, place the jar in an area where it will receive an abundance of sunlight. As night falls, the jar will come to life with a galaxy type appearance.

Beach Mason Jar Terrarium

Materials:

- Mason jar
- Sand
- Seashells
- Driftwood (optional)
- Seaglass (optional)
- Washi tape

Directions:

Step 1: Wrap a piece of washi tape around the ring of the mason jar. This gives the jar a more decorative look. You can, however, skip this step if you like.

Step 2: Pour sand into the jar. The amount you use depends on your preference. A good general rule of thumb is to fill the jar about 2/3 full with sand.

Step 3: Place the seashells and other beach finds in the jar.

Step 4: Place the lid on top of the mason jar and screw the ring down. You now have a awesome beach terrarium!

Kid-Friendly Moss Terrarium

Materials:

- Mason jar
- Small pebbles
- Potting soil
- Activated charcoal
- Moss
- Small plants (optional)
- Bamboo skewer
- Larger rocks for decoration (optional)

Directions:

Step 1: Cover the bottom 1-inch of the mason jar with small pebbles. This creates a false drainage system.

Step 2: Place a thin layer of the activated charcoal on top of the pebbles. This helps to prevent bacteria and fungus buildup while keeping the water fresh.

Step 3: Apply a layer of soil on top of the charcoal. Potting soil is the best choice but the soil from your yard will also work.

Step 4: Poke small holes into the soil. Insert the moss and small plants into the holes. You can position the plants how you like in the jar. A good general rule of thumb, however, is to place the larger plants in the back.

Step 5: Position the rocks in the jar if desired.

Mason Jar Aquarium

Materials:

- Mason jar
- Blue food coloring
- Distilled water
- Plastic sea creature figurines
- Plastic plants
- Aquarium gravel
- White and blue glitter
- Liquid glycerin

Directions:

Step 1: Pour about a 1-inch layer of aquarium gravel on the bottom of the mason jar.

Step 2: In a separate glass jar, mix the distilled water with a few drops of blue food coloring.

Step 3: Carefully pour the colored distilled water into the mason jar. Add a bit of white and blue glitter into the water.

Step 4: Add a drop of liquid glycerin. This helps to slow down the glitter when it's falling.

Step 5: Add a bit of white and blue glitter into the water.

Step 6: Place the plastic plants and sea creature figurines in the water.

Step 7: Secure the ring and lid on the jar. You know have your own portable aquarium!

Chapter 6 – Holiday and Seasonal Mason Jar Crafts

Easter Treat Jars

Materials:

- Mason jar
- Edible Easter grass
- Egg-shaped chocolate candies, M&Ms in pastel colors or jellybeans
- Chocolate bunny
- Decorate Easter ribbon

Directions:

Step 1: Fill the bottom of the mason jar with edible Easter grass.

Step 2: Pour some egg-shaped chocolate candies, M&Ms in pastel colors or jellybeans.

Step 3: Unwrap the chocolate bunny. Set it in the middle of the mason jar.

Step 4: Secure the lid close and tie a decorate ribbon around the rim of the mason jar.

Tip: If making more than one of these Easter treat jars, consider attach a decorative tag to the ribbon with the recipient's name written on it.

Halloween Boo Mason Jar Luminaries

Materials:

- 3 quart-sized mason jars
- Flameless tea lights
- Frosted glass spray paint
- Glitter Blast Diamond Dust spray paint
- Sponge brush
- 1 two-inch "B" alphabet sticker
- 2 two-inch "O" alphabet stickers
- Black matte paint
- Twine
- Halloween embellishments, such as fake spiders, fake bats, exctra

Directions:

Step 1: Place the "B" sticker on one of the mason jars. Do the same with the "O" stickers on the two other mason jars.

Step 2: Paint the entire exterior of the jars with the frosted glass spray paint. Let the paint dry completely before continuing.

Step 3: Paint the mason jars with the Glitter Blast Diamond Dust spray paint. Let dry completely before continuing.

Step 4: While the spray paint is drying, paint the lids and rings of the mason jars black and let dry.

Step 5: Carefully peel the alphabet stickers off the mason jars.

Step 6: Tie twine around the top of each mason jar and secure it with a decorative knot or bow.

Step 7: If desired, attach fake spiders or small plastic bats to the jar for an added Halloweenish appearance.

Step 8: Place 1 flameless tea light candle in each mason jar. Secure the lid and ring onto each jar and place in the desired location for a spooky effect.

Decorative Fall Mason Jar Candle Holder

Materials:

- Mason jar
- Leaves (fake or real)
- Mod Podge
- Sponge brush
- Twine or decorative ribbon
- Tea candle

Directions:

Step 1: Paint the Mod Podge onto the back of a leaf with the sponge brush.

Step 2: Press the glue-covered leaf onto the mason jar. Continue in this manner until you have covered the entire exterior of the mason jar with leaves.

Sep 3: Let the glue dry completely before tying the twine or ribbon around the top of the jar and into a bow.

Step 4: Set the candle in the middle of the jar. Light when ready.

Simple Yet Elegant Winter Mason Jar Candle Holder

Materials:

- Mason jar
- Twine
- Epsom salt
- Tea light or small candle

Directions:

Step 1: Wrap twine around the mouth of the mason jar several times. Secure the twine in place with a decorative knot.

Step 2: Pour Epsom salt into the mason jar until it is about 2/3 full. You can adjust the amount of salt used based on your desires and the height of the candles.

Step 3: Insert the candle into the middle of the mason jar. Press it into the salt to keep it sturdy.

Step 4: Place the mason jar candle holder in the desired location and light when ready.

Pine and Pinecone Mason Jar Candle Holders

Materials:

- Mason jars
- Epsom salt
- Pinecones
- White acrylic paint
- Sponge brush
- Ribbon or twine
- Tealight candles
- Fresh pine
- Hot glue gun and glue sticks

Directions:

Step 1: Paint the tips of the pinecone with white paint. You want to create the appearance of "snow" on the tips of the pinecones. Let the paint dry completely.

Step 2: Place some fresh pine in the bottom of the mason jar. Sprinkle Epsom salt over the pine. The Epsom salt will make it appear as if there is snow in the mason jar.

Step 3: Place a candle in the middle of the mason jar.

Step 4: Wrap ribbon or twine around the top of the mason jar. Tie the ribbon in a decorate bow.

Step 5: Use the hot glue gun to secure the pinecones onto the ribbon.

Step 6: Light the candle when ready to create a warm atmosphere.

Chapter 7– Don't Forget the Lid: Crafts Using only Mason Jar Lids

While most people think the mason jar lid is useful for nothing more than keeping the jar sealed, they are completely wrong. That innocent-looking lid can be upcycled into a wide array of projects for your home.

Keep in mind, however, that certain mason jar lid projects require a center type of lid. There are generally two types of mason jar lids. The first type is the most common used today and consists of two pieces, a lid and a ring. The lid is placed on top of the jar and the ring is screwed down onto the jar keeping the lid in place. The second lid is generally seen now-a-days on smaller mason jars – such as jelly jars – and is simply your common one-piece lid.

If the craft project calls for the one-piece mason jar lid, and all you have are the two-piece types, don't fret! You can simply turn the two-piece into a one-piece by gluing the lid to the ring.

DIY Picture Magnets

Materials:

- Lids and rings from mason jars
- Cardboard
- Pictures
- Mod Podge
- Sponge brush
- Craft glue
- 1-inch magnet disks
- Washi tape
- Pencil
- Scissors or x-acto knife

Directions:

Step 1: Secure the lid to the mason jar rings with craft glue. Let dry for a few hours before continuing.

Step 2: Place the lid upside down on a piece of thin cardboard. Trace around the lid with a pencil. Cut the circle out of the cardboard.

Step 3: Place the cardboard circle over the area of the picture you want shown. Trace around the cardboard. Cut the circle out of the picture.

Step 3: Push the cardboard circle into the inside of the lid.

Step 4: Paint the Mod Podge over top the circle-shaped picture. Let dry.

Step5: Apply a few dots of craft glue to the back of the circle-shaped picture. Press the picture onto the circle-shaped cardboard that is inside the lid. Let dry.

Step 6: Cover the sides of the lid with washi tape. Glue the magnet disk to the back of the lid. Let dry.

Step 7: Place the magnet picture frame on the fridge.

Tip: You can eliminate the ring portion of the mason jar if desired and merely use the lid.

Mason Jar Lid Candles

Materials:

- Mason jar 1 piece lids, not the lids that require rings
- Wax, pastilles
- Thermometer
- Wicks
- Scents, optional

Directions:

Step1: Add the wax pastilles to a double boiler and melt while stirring continuously. Remove the wax from heat once completely melted. If using scents, stir them into the wax now.

Step 2: Carefully pour the melted wax into the lids. Let sit for 4 minutes.

Step 3: Place the wicks into the middle of the wax-filled mason jar lids. To help keep the wicks standing upright, place a skewer across the edge of the mason jar lid.

Step 4: Let the wax cool for about an hour. After the allotted time, trim the wick to ¼-inch.

Birdseed Feeder

Materials:

- Mason jar lid
- ¼ cup water
- ¾ cup birdseed
- Knox gelatin, 1 small envelope
- String or twine
- Wax paper

Directions:

Step 1: Pour the water in a small pan and place on the stove.

Step 2: Add the gelatin and mix while heating the water to a simmer.

Step 3: Remove the mixture from heat and stir in the birdseed.

Step 4: Lay the mason jars on a piece of wax paper. You want the top of the lid to be laying flat on the wax paper.

Step 5: Spoon a bit of the birdseed mixture into the lid. Press the mixture into the lid with your fingers.

Step 6: Tie the string or twin into a loop. Lay the loop directly on the birdseed mixture. Fill the remaining lid with the birdseed, pressing it into the lid with your fingers.

Step 7: Allow the birdseed to dry overnight. Once dry, carefully flip the lid over and shake the birdfeeder out.

Step 8: Hang the birdfeeder outside where your feathered friends can enjoy it.

Garden Markers

Materials:

- Mason jar lids only
- Wooden dowels
- White spray paint
- Acrylic paint
- Paint brushes
- Clear coat spray paint
- Hot glue gun and glue sticks
- Permanent marker

Directions:

Step 1: Spray the jar lid with the white spray paint. You are doing this create a clean surface for you to paint on. Let the paint dry completely before continuing.

Step 2: Paint the lids with the desired design. Go crazy and have fun! You don't have to use only one or two colors of acrylic paint; you can use every color in the rainbow if you like.

Step 3: Let the paint dry before continuing.

Step 4: Neatly write the name of the plant on the lid with the permanent marker.

Step 5: Apply a generous amount of hot glue to the back of the painted lid. Press the side of the wooden dowel into the hot glue. Apply more glue, covering the area of the dowel that is touching the lid. Let the hot glue dry for several hours.

Step 6: When ready to use, press the garden marker into the soil of the corresponding plant.

Natural Suncatcher Wind Chime

Materials:

- Mason jar rings
- Contact paper
- Scissors
- Flowers and leaves
- Marker
- Twine
- Sturdy stick

Directions:

Step 1: Lay a sheet of contact paper on a flat surface. Trace around the mason jar ring onto the paper with the marker. Make sure you are tracing on the side that doesn't peel off. Continue tracing until you have the same amount of circles as you do rings.

Step 2: Carefully remove the backing from the contact paper. Let the sticky part of the contact paper lay on the flat surface. Make sure the sticky part is facing up.

Step 3: Place the flowers and leaves into the circles you created. Get creative! The stickiness of the contact paper will keep the flowers and leaves in place.

Step 4: Remove the backing from another piece of contact paper. Lay the sticky side down on top of the first piece of contact paper. Press the paper down flat around the items.

Step 5: Cut the circles out from the contact paper with a pair of scissors.

Step 6: Tie a piece of twin around the rings and secure with a knot.

Step 7: Press the circle into the mason jar ring.

Step 8: Tie the other end of the twine to a sturdy stick.

Step 9: Hang the suncatcher on your porch, patio or wherever you desire.

Mason Jar Lids Christmas Ornament

Materials:

- Mason jar lids
- Mod Podge
- Sponge brush
- Wrapping paper
- Sheet music
- Pages from old books
- Thin ribbon or thread
- Nail
- Hammer
- Paper hole punch

Directions:

Step 1: Create a hole in the lid by carefully hammering a nail at the top edge of the lid.

Step 2: Carefully cut the wrapping paper, sheet music and/or pages from an old book so that it will fit snugly into the mason jar lid.

Step 3: Brush a thin layer of Mod Podge onto the front of the wrapping paper, sheet music and/or pages from an old book. Let dry for 15 minutes before applying a second layer. Let dry completely before continuing.

Step 4: Press the Mod Podge-covered wrapping paper, sheet music and/or pages from an old book into the mason jar lid.

Step 5: Use a paper hole punch to create a hole into the paper. Make sure you create the new hole so that it lines up with the hole created in Step 1.

Step 6: Feed thin ribbon or thread through the holes and tie with a knot. Hang the ornament from your tree.

Conclusion

Remember that the mason jar projects discussed above are not set in stone. This means you can alter them as you see fit. The most important thing to remember is to make the crafts your own and have fun with the mason jars! If you're not having a good time creating the projects then what is the sense in doing it?

Furthermore, if you fail at a mason jar craft project, don't give up! The age-old saying, "if at first you don't succeed, try, try again" is something that all crafters must take to heart. Not every project you start will be a success and you will probably experience more fails then you would like to admit. But with failure comes knowledge. And this knowledge can help you succeed with your future craft projects.

Made in the USA
Columbia, SC
05 January 2020